Learning How to Learn

Tools for schools

Mary James, Paul Black,
Patrick Carmichael, Colin Conner,
Peter Dudley, Alison Fox, David Frost,
Leslie Honour, John MacBeath,
Robert McCormick, Bethan Marshall,
David Pedder, Richard Procter,
Sue Swaffield and Dylan Wiliam

Routledge
Taylor & Francis Group

LONDON AND NEW YORK

TLRP Improving Practice Series

Series Editor: Andrew Pollard, Director of the ESRC Teaching and Learning Programme

Learning How to Learn: tools for schools

Mary James, Paul Black, Patrick Carmichael, Colin Conner, Peter Dudley, Alison Fox, David Frost, Leslie Honour, John MacBeath, Robert McCormick, Bethan Marshall, David Pedder, Richard Procter, Sue Swaffield and Dylan Wiliam

First published 2006
by Routledge
2 Park Square, Milton Park, Abingdon, Oxon OX14 4RN

Simultaneously published in the USA and Canada
by Routledge
270 Madison Ave, New York, NY 10016

Routledge is an imprint of the Taylor & Francis Group, an informa business

© 2006 Mary James, Paul Black, Patrick Carmichael, Colin Conner, Peter Dudley, Alison Fox, David Frost, Leslie Honour, John MacBeath, Robert McCormick, Bethan Marshall, David Pedder, Richard Procter, Sue Swaffield and Dylan Wiliam

Typeset in Melior and Futura by Keystroke, 28 High Street, Tettenhall, Wolverhampton
Printed and bound in Great Britain by Bell & Bain Ltd, Glasgow

British Library Cataloguing in Publication Data
A catalogue record for this book is available from the British Library

Library of Congress Cataloging in Publication Data
Learning how to learn : tools for schools / Mary James ... [et al.].
p. cm.
1. Learning. 2. Learning strategies. 3. Teachers–In-service training.
I. James, Mary.
LB1060.L3824 2006
370.15'23–dc22   2005034859

ISBN10: 0–415–40026–0 (pbk)
ISBN10: 0–203–96717–8 (ebk)

ISBN13: 978–0–415–40026–8 (pbk)
ISBN13: 978–0–203–96717–1 (ebk)

Contents

Preface

The ideas for *Improving Practice* contained in this book are underpinned by high quality research from the Teaching and Learning Research Programme (TLRP), the UK's largest ever coordinated investment in education enquiry. Each suggestion has been tried and tested with experienced practitioners and has been found to improve learning outcomes – particularly if the underlying principles about Teaching and Learning have been understood. The key, then, remains the exercise of professional judgement, knowledge and skill. We hope that the *Improving Practice* series will encourage and support teachers in exploring new ways of enhancing learning experiences and improving educational outcomes of all sorts. For future information about TLRP, and additional 'practitioner applications', see www.tlrp.org.

Acknowledgements

We are very grateful to the teachers and pupils in the forty infant, primary and secondary schools, and the advisers in Essex, Hertfordshire, Medway, Oxfordshire and Redbridge local authorities, and the Kent and Somerset VEAZ, who worked closely with us on the Learning How to Learn Project. We have learned a great deal from them and we owe much to their generosity in sharing their time, their ideas and their experience with us.

We also thank the many other individuals and organisations who supported us in different ways.

This book is based on the work of 'Learning How to Learn – in classrooms, schools and networks', a four-year development and research project funded from January 2001 to July 2005 by the UK Economic and Social Research Council as part of Phase II of the Teaching and Learning Research Programme. The Project (ref: L139 25 1020) was directed by Mary James (who was at Cambridge University until December 2004, then at the Institute of Education, London) and co-directed, from 2002, by Robert McCormick (Open University). Other members of the research team were Patrick Carmichael, Mary-Jane Drummond, John MacBeath, David Pedder, Richard Procter and Sue Swaffield (University of Cambridge), Paul Black and Bethan Marshall (King's College London), Leslie Honour (University of Reading) and Alison Fox (Open University). Past members of the team were Geoff Southworth, University of Reading (until March 2002), Colin Conner and David Frost, University of Cambridge (until April 2003 and April 2004 respectively) and Dylan Wiliam and Joanna Swann, King's College London (until August 2003 and January 2005 respectively). Pete Dudley and Robin Bevan were ESRC TLRP research training fellows, linked to the project, and Carmel Casey-Morley and Nichola Daily were project administrators, based at Cambridge. Further details are available at http://www.learntolearn.ac.uk.

About this book

Learning how to learn through assessment for learning

We have written this practical book to provide schools with resources to help their teachers develop the principles and practices associated with assessment for learning (AfL) and learning how to learn (LHTL). Teachers who develop in this way can help pupils to become autonomous, independent learners, which is at the heart of learning how to learn – a crucial aspect of learning in the fast-moving world of the twenty-first century.

There has been a huge growth of interest in assessment for learning in recent years because it re-orientates assessment practices to serve formative purposes – to use them to *improve* learning, not just measure it. Of central importance are practices that:

- help learners to understand learning objectives and to know what counts as high-quality learning;
- help learners to build on strengths and overcome barriers in their previous learning;
- help learners to know how to act on constructive feedback about how to improve, and develop the motivation to do so;
- help learners to use the help of others, including through peer-assessment, to enhance their understanding and take responsibility for their own learning.

These practices are all about making the processes and practices of learning explicit to learners and encouraging them to take control of them. In this sense they are about the wider concept of 'learning how to learn'. We have come to understand this not as a specific 'ability', but as a set of 'practices and strategies' that learners can engage in to enhance their learning. Neither do we see it as in some way detached from learning 'something' in a subject area. Learning how to learn and learning something are bound up together: the former are ways of going about the latter. We would caution against separate LHTL lessons because learning how to learn needs to be developed in context. Therefore all teachers need to engage with it.

The book is also based on the idea that successful learning by pupils in schools depends in large measure on the quality of teaching they experience. Innovations in teaching associated with AfL and LHTL often require teachers to change their behaviour, their perceptions of their roles, and, sometimes, their beliefs and values. In order for these changes to take place, teachers themselves need to learn, and the schools in which they work need to support their professional development. This requires organisational learning and sharing ideas about practice within schools and across networks of schools.

We provide tools and advice for teachers, schools, advisers and teacher educators to use in support of teachers' learning and in the self-evaluation and development of schools and networks of schools. We expect that these materials will be particularly useful as resources for professional development activities. However, the book is not intended as a prescription about what should be done but as a source of ideas that both primary and secondary schools can use, and adapt, to suit their circumstances and their analyses of their particular needs. It draws on the in-service materials and some of the research instruments that were generated in a major development and research project: 'Learning How to Learn – in classrooms, schools and networks' (see the Appendix on pages 103–105 for details).

As the research evidence on the effectiveness of assessment for learning has demonstrated, the development of learning how to learn holds much promise for enhancing the process of learning and improving outcomes for all learners. There is nothing in schools that can be more important.

How this book is organised

The book is organised in four main parts:

Part I – Getting started, which provides:
- an article about the meaning and evidence for assessment for learning;
- an introductory presentation outlining the evidence for AfL and the practices that schools have used to support the development of LHTL through AfL;
- two alternative routes to deciding how to take work forward in schools:
  - an audit and action-planning activity to use following the introductory INSET;
  - a staff questionnaire (A) about classroom assessment practices and values which can be used as a self-evaluation tool to identify areas in need of development.

Part II – Going deeper, which provides:
- four workshops, which are intended to provide more background and activities to develop some of the practices identified in the initial INSET session:
  - developing classroom talk through questioning;
  - appropriate feedback;
  - sharing criteria of quality with learners;
  - self-assessment and peer-assessment;
- a fifth workshop on 'How people learn'. This was written as a response to schools and teachers who wanted to get up to date with learning theory because they appreciated that this was a foundation for AfL and LHTL.

Part III – Learning across and beyond the school, which provides:
- two further staff questionnaires for use as school self-evaluation instruments:
  - B – on teachers' professional learning, practices and values;
  - C – on school management systems, practices and values;
- a set of tools for the development of learning at school level;
- a network-mapping tool for exploring connections within and across schools to enhance knowledge creation and transfer.

Part IV – Developing and sharing practice, which provides:
- an account of in-school adaptation of a specific practice – the use of 'traffic lights' – to suit different schools' particular circumstances;
- ideas about how to promote between-school collaboration and development.

Although we were constrained to structure these resources in a linear fashion, we expect that schools will want to use them in different ways according to their starting points and their analyses of their particular needs. Thus we have tried to make the activities as self-contained as possible. For example, we have included references and further reading in the text of the activities rather than provide a bibliography at the end of this book.

We encourage teachers, and those who support their learning, to photocopy material that they wish to use with colleagues for professional development, although we expect the source to be fully acknowledged.

Part I   Getting started

Overview

This section begins with a short article 'Assessment for learning: what it is and what research says about it' (see pages 7–13). This is intended as background reading for the school's professional development co-ordinator, or relevant group, but may be given to all teachers as a handout to accompany an introductory INSET session. Some teachers may feel that they are familiar with these ideas, although our experience suggests that many misunderstandings still abound: for instance, formative assessment is often confused with frequent mini-summative assessments. This article may help to clarify the central role of AfL in teaching and learning. It also provides all the references to source material that are used in the introductory presentation that follows.

The presentation, 'Learning how to learn through assessment for learning' (see pages 15–18) is given here in the form of copies of sixteen slides. This could be used as the basis of a talk to teachers at the beginning of a programme of professional development. The presentation has two parts. The first eleven slides provide a rationale for making assessment for learning a focus for innovation and change in teachers' classroom practice. These outline the key components – dialogue and questioning, feedback, sharing criteria, and peer- and self-assessment – and what research says about their effectiveness in improving learning. In our experience it is a good idea to allow group discussion of this evidence before moving on. The remaining slides provide ideas, drawn from a number of AfL projects, about practices that might fruitfully be implemented in schools. These slides also emphasise the key learning principles that underpin the practices. A PowerPoint version of these slides, and another version with less detail on the slides but more in accompanying notes, can be downloaded from our website at http://www.learntolearn.ac.uk.

Each school will need to decide how to proceed with development following such a presentation. On its own it is unlikely to be sufficient to stimulate fruitful activity, so it needs to be incorporated into a comprehensive plan for more sustained professional development. This should have two elements: opportunities for teachers to learn together and opportunities for them to develop practice in their own classrooms. Classroom learning can then be brought back to the teachers' group for further reflection, critique and refinement – an action research sequence.

Activity can be initiated in a number of different ways and two suggestions are offered here. The first is an audit and action-planning activity (page 19) that can be used directly after the initial presentation. This asks teachers to reflect on the introductory presentation and decide where they want to go next. On the assumption that not all of what they have heard will be novel, they are asked, first, to note the practices they already carry out and how these might be strengthened. Then they are asked to identify new practices that they wish to try out. The strain of adding to existing workload is acknowledged, so teachers are also asked to consider practices, currently engaged in, which are less productive of learning and might be reduced. Excessive but habitual forms of record-keeping are sometimes identified in this category. The rest of the activity follows familiar conventions for action planning. This activity is easily photocopied but the sheet is also available to download from the website.

The second route to deciding a strategy for development involves more systematic data collection and analysis using a self-evaluation questionnaire (see pages 20–24) based on thirty statements about classroom assessment practices. The questionnaire can be photocopied from the materials given here or it can be downloaded from the website. You may wish to do your own analysis of the responses in ways that suit your purposes. However, if more help is needed, a spreadsheet can be downloaded from the website.

Schools usually find item level data of great interest because the questions focus on particular classroom practices and can reveal differences in values and practice across categories of staff, e.g. classroom teachers, managers and classroom assistants, across older and newer teachers, or across subjects. However, common patterns of response to *groups* of questions (factors) can also be important to think about. For classroom assessment practices we have identified three factors which may be of interest to schools in analysing their own results. The following tables list the items that make up these factors and give an indication of the kinds of values–practice gaps that were found by aggregating the results from over 500 classroom teachers in 32 'average' primary and secondary schools. 'Values' were assessed by asking teachers how important they felt these practices to be, and 'practices' were assessed by asking teachers whether they carried them out. These tables may provide some basis for comparison with responses in your school. This provides a starting point, although there are dangers in simply comparing percentages and it may be better to compare means and standard deviations to measure differences with greater accuracy. Schools that wish to do this will probably need to use a statistics software package or the spreadsheet on our website.

Factor A1: Making learning explicit

Eliciting, clarifying and responding to evidence of learning; working with pupils to develop a positive learning orientation

Item		Values (%) Important/ crucial	Practices (%) Often/ mostly true
1	Assessment provides me with useful evidence of pupils' understandings that I use to plan subsequent lessons.	96	92
10	Pupils are told how well they have done in relation to their own previous performance.	98	88
11	Pupils' learning objectives are discussed with pupils in ways they understand.	98	94
14	I identify pupils' strengths and advise them on how to develop them further.	99	88
15	Pupils are helped to find ways of addressing problems they have in their learning.	99	86
16	Pupils are encouraged to view mistakes as valuable learning opportunities.	97	87
18	I use questions mainly to elicit reasons and explanations from my pupils.	94	91
20	Pupils' errors are valued for the insights they reveal about how pupils are thinking.	88	81
21	Pupils are helped to understand the learning purposes of each lesson or series of lessons.	96	90
27	Pupil effort is seen as important when assessing their learning.	92	90

Factor A2: Promoting learning autonomy

A widening of scope for pupils to take on greater independence over their learning objectives and the assessment of their own and each other's work

Item		Values (%) Important/ crucial	Practices (%) Often/ mostly true
6	Pupils are given opportunities to decide their own learning objectives.	65	31
13	I provide guidance to help pupils assess their own work.	95	74
19	I provide guidance to help pupils to assess one another's work.	73	51
24	I provide guidance to help pupils assess their own learning.	93	69
29	Pupils are given opportunities to assess one another's work.	72	47

Factor A3: Performance orientation

A concern to help pupils comply with performance goals prescribed by the curriculum through closed questioning and measured by marks and grades

Item		Values (%) Important/ crucial	Practices (%) Often/ mostly true
2	The next lesson is determined more by the prescribed curriculum than by how well pupils did in the last lesson.	51	57
3	The main emphasis in my assessments is on whether pupils know, understand or can do prescribed elements of the curriculum.	90	96
7	I use questions mainly to elicit factual knowledge from my pupils.	57	66
8	I consider the most worthwhile assessment to be assessment that is undertaken by the teacher.	67	71
12	Assessment of pupils' work consists primarily of marks and grades.	35	47
23	Pupils' learning objectives are determined mainly by the prescribed curriculum.	63	92

When analysing questionnaire results, patterns of similarity or difference might be helpful in deciding where to put the main effort in developing practice in school. For example, you might find that making learning explicit through sharing learning objectives is common practice, but allowing pupils to identify their own learning objectives is underdeveloped.

There are other classroom-level research instruments on the project website, which are available to download, and may help you to examine certain issues in more depth. For example there are students' beliefs about, and attitudes to, learning questionnaires, for various age groups, and a teachers' beliefs about learning questionnaire. We had no space to reproduce these in this book but teachers might find them useful as self-evaluation tools.

Background reading

What follows is the short summary article, 'Assessment for learning: what it is and what research says about it', which provides background to assessment for learning research and practice. It will be useful for anyone who leads professional development in this area as it provides more detail on the slides that are used in the presentation (see pages 15–18). As mentioned earlier, INSET leaders may choose to give copies to teachers to read either before or shortly after the first session in the professional development programme they plan.

Assessment for learning: what it is and what research says about it

What is assessment for learning?

It would be quite reasonable for any teacher to ask, with a degree of puzzlement, why something called assessment for learning (AfL) has moved centre stage in the drive to improve teaching and learning. The past experience of many teachers, pupils and their parents has been of assessment as something that happens *after* teaching and learning. The idea that assessment can be an integral part of teaching and learning requires a significant shift in our thinking but this is precisely what assessment for learning implies. So, before we look at what research on AfL can tell us, it is important to understand what it is.

The nature of assessment

It is no accident that the word 'assessment' comes from a Latin word meaning 'to sit beside' because a central feature of assessment is the close observation of what one person says or does by another, or, in the case of self-assessment, reflection on one's own knowledge, understanding or behaviour. This is true of the whole spectrum of assessments, from formal tests and examinations to informal assessments made by teachers in their classrooms many hundred times each day. Although the *form* that assessments take may be very different – some may be pencil and paper tests whilst others may be based on questioning in normal classroom interactions – all assessments have some common characteristics. They all involve: (i) making observations; (ii) interpreting the evidence; (iii) making judgements that can be used for decisions about actions.

OBSERVATION

In order to carry out assessment, it is necessary to find out what pupils know and can do or the difficulties they are experiencing. Observation of regular classroom activity, such as listening to talk, watching pupils engaged in tasks, or reviewing the products of their class work and homework, may provide the information needed, but on other occasions it may be necessary to elicit the information needed in a very deliberate and specific way. A task or test might serve this purpose but a carefully chosen oral question can be just as effective. Pupils' responses to tasks or questions then need to be interpreted. In other words, the assessor needs to work out what the evidence means.

INTERPRETATION

Interpretations are made with reference to what is of interest such as specific skills, attitudes or different kinds of knowledge. These are often referred to as criteria and relate to learning goals or objectives. Usually observations as part of assessment are made with these criteria in mind, i.e. formulated beforehand, but sometimes teachers observe unplanned interactions or outcomes and apply criteria retrospectively. Interpretations can describe or attempt to explain a behaviour, or they can infer from a behaviour, e.g. what a child says, that something is going on inside a child's head, e.g. thinking. For this reason interpretations are sometimes called inferences.

JUDGEMENT

On the basis of these interpretations of evidence, judgements are made. These involve evaluations. It is at this point that the assessment process looks rather different according to the different purposes it is expected to serve and the uses to which the information will be put.

Different purposes

A distinction between formative and summative (summing-up) purposes has been familiar since the 1960s, although the meaning of these two terms has not been well understood. A more transparent distinction, meaning roughly the same thing, is between assessment *of* learning, for grading and reporting, and assessment *for* learning, where the explicit purpose is to use assessment as part of teaching to promote pupils' learning. AfL becomes 'formative' when evidence is actually used to adapt teaching and learning practices to meet learning needs. AfL came to prominence, as a concept, after the publication in 1999 of a pamphlet with this title by the Assessment Reform Group, a small group of UK academics who have worked, since 1989, to bring evidence from research to the attention of teachers and policymakers.

ASSESSMENT FOR LEARNING

In AfL, observations, interpretations and criteria may be similar to those employed in assessment *of* learning, but the nature of *judgements* and *decisions* that flow from them will be different. In essence, AfL focuses on what is revealed about where children are in their learning, especially the nature of, and reasons for, the strengths and weaknesses they exhibit. AfL judgements are therefore concerned with what they might do to move forward.

The Assessment Reform Group (2002a) gave this definition of AfL:

> Assessment for Learning is the process of seeking and interpreting evidence for use by learners and their teachers to decide where the learners are in their learning, where they need to go and how best to get there.

One significant element of this definition is the emphasis on learners' use of evidence. This draws attention to the fact that teachers are not the only assessors. Pupils can be involved in peer- and self-assessment and, even when teachers are heavily involved, pupils need to be actively engaged. Only learners can do the learning, so they need to act upon information and feedback if their learning is to improve. This requires them to have understanding, but also the motivation and will, to act. The implications for teaching and learning practices are profound and far-reaching.

ASSESSMENT OF LEARNING

In contrast, the main purpose of assessment *of* learning is to sum up what a pupil has learned at a given point. As such it is not designed to contribute directly to future learning although high-stakes testing can have a powerful negative impact (Assessment Reform Group, 2002b). In assessment of learning, the judgement will explicitly compare a pupil's performance with an agreed standard or with the standards achieved by a group of pupils of, say, the same age. The judgement may then be in the form of 'has/has not' met the standard or, more usually, on a scale represented as scores or levels. These are symbolic shorthand for the criteria and standards that underpin them. Representation in this concise, but sometimes cryptic, way is convenient when there is a need to report to other people such as parents, receiving teachers at transition points, and managers interested in monitoring the system at school, local and national level. Reporting, selection and monitoring are therefore prominent uses of this kind of assessment information.

CAN SUMMATIVE DATA BE USED FORMATIVELY?

Scores and levels, especially when aggregated across groups of pupils, are often referred to as 'data' although any information, systematically collected, can be referred to in this way. Aggregated summative data are useful for identifying patterns of performance and alerting teachers to groups that are performing above or below expectations. However, schools need to investigate further if they are to discover the reasons for these patterns in order to plan what to do. Similarly, at the level of the individual pupil, summative judgements are helpful in indicating levels of achievement and, by implication, the next levels that need to be aimed for if learners are to make progress. However, scores and levels need to be 'unpacked' to reveal the evidence and criteria they refer to if they are to make any contribution to helping pupils to take these next steps. What is important is the qualitative information about the underlying features of a performance that can be used in feedback to pupils. For example, telling a child that he has achieved a Level 4 will not help him to know what to do to achieve a Level 5, although exploring with him the features of his work that led to this judgement, and explaining aspects of it that he might improve, could help him to know what to do to make progress. In this context the summative judgement (in number form) is stripped away and the teacher goes back to the evidence (observation and interpretation) on which it was made. She then makes a formative judgement (in words) about what the evidence says about where the learner is, where he needs to go, and how he might best get there.

By changing the nature of the judgement, assessments designed originally for summative purposes may be converted into assessments *for* learning. However, not having been designed to elicit evidence that will contribute directly to learning, they may be less suited to that purpose than assessments designed with AfL in mind. External tests are even more problematic than summative teacher assessments, because teachers rarely have access to enough of the evidence on which scores and levels are based, although analyses of common errors can be useful.

What does research say about how to improve assessment for learning?

The key text is the review of research by Paul Black and Dylan Wiliam (1998a, 1998b), which was commissioned by the Assessment Reform Group. This reviews research carried out across the world, in many sectors of education and subject areas, from 1987 to 1997. It also refers to two previous reviews of research (Natriello, 1987; Crooks, 1988). The summary below draws on this work, and adds some insights from studies carried out since 1998.

Black and Wiliam analysed 250 studies of which 50 were a particular focus because they provided evidence of gains in achievement after 'interventions' based on what we might now call AfL practices. These gains, measured by pre- and post-summative tests, produced standardised effect sizes of between 0.4 and 0.7. An effect size of 0.4 would move the average student up half a level at Key Stage 2; an effect size of 0.7 would move them up three-quarters of a level. An effect size of 0.7 for secondary school pupils could mean gains of between one and two grades at GCSE. There was evidence that gains for lower-attaining students were even greater. These findings have convinced many teachers and policymakers that AfL is worth taking seriously.

The innovations introduced into classroom practice involved some combination of the following:

Developing classroom talk and questioning

Asking questions, either orally or in writing, is crucial to the process of eliciting information about the current state of a pupil's understanding. However, questions phrased simply to establish whether pupils know the correct answer are of little value for formative purposes. Pupils can give right answers for the wrong reasons, or wrong answers for very understandable reasons. For example, Vinner (1997) showed that pupils gave very different answers to superficially similar questions on fractions in mathematics. When the pupils were asked to talk through how they had reached their answers it emerged that many pupils developed a naïve conception (a rule of thumb) that large fractions have small denominators and small fractions have large denominators. This rule often serves them well and their teachers may be unaware of the misconception. Thus, if learning is to be secure, superficially 'correct' answers need to be probed and misconceptions explored. In this way pupils' learning needs can be diagnosed.

Recent research in science education, by Millar and Hames (2003), has shown how carefully designed diagnostic 'probes' can provide quality information of pupils' understanding to inform subsequent action. The implication is that teachers need to spend time planning good diagnostic questions, possibly with colleagues. Pupils can be trained to ask questions too, and to reflect on answers. They need thinking time to do this, as they do to formulate answers that go beyond the superficial. Increasing thinking time, between asking a question and taking an answer, from the average of 0.9 of a second, can be productive in this respect. So can a 'no hands up' rule which implies that all pupils can be called upon to answer and that their answers will be dealt with seriously, whether right or wrong.

All these ideas call for changes in the norms of talk in many classrooms. By promoting thoughtful and sustained dialogue, teachers can explore the knowledge and understanding of pupils and build on this. The principle of 'contingent teaching' underpins this aspect of AfL.

Giving appropriate feedback

Feedback is always important but it needs to be approached cautiously because research draws attention to potential negative effects. Kluger and DeNisi (1996) reviewed 131 studies of feedback and found that, in two out of five studies, giving people feedback made their performance worse. Further investigation revealed that this happened when feedback focused on their self-esteem or self-image, as is the case when marks are given, or when praise focuses on the person rather than the learning. Praise can make pupils feel good but it does not help their learning unless it is explicit about what the pupil has done well.

This point is powerfully reinforced by research by Butler (1988) who compared the effects of giving marks as numerical scores, comments only, and marks plus comments. Pupils given only comments made 30 per cent progress and all were motivated. No gains were made by those given marks or those given marks plus comments. In both these groups the lower achievers also lost interest. The explanation was that giving marks washed out the beneficial effects of the comments. Careful commenting works best when it stands on its own.

Another study, by Day and Cordón (1993), found that there is no need for teachers to give complete solutions when pupils 'get stuck'. Indeed, Year 4 pupils retained their learning longer when they were simply given an indication of where they should be looking for a solution (a 'scaffolded' response). This encouraged them to adopt a 'mindful' approach and active involvement, which rarely happens when teachers 'correct' pupils' work.

Sharing criteria with learners

Research also shows how important it is that pupils understand what counts as success in different curriculum areas and at different stages in their development as learners. This entails sharing learning 'intentions, expectations, objectives, goals, targets' (these words tend to be used interchangeably) and 'success criteria'. However, because these are often framed in generalised ways, they are rarely enough on their own. Pupils need to see what they mean, as applied in the context of their own work, or that of others. They will not understand criteria right away, but regular discussions of concrete examples will help pupils' develop understandings of quality. According to Sadler (1989):

> The indispensable conditions for improvement are that the *student* comes to hold a concept of quality roughly similar to that held by the teacher, is able to monitor continuously the quality of what is being produced *during the act of production itself*, and has a repertoire of alternative moves or strategies from which to draw at any given point. In other words, students have to be able to judge the quality of what they are producing and be able to regulate what they are doing during the doing of it.

In a context where creativity is valued, as well as excellence, it is important to see criteria of quality as representing a 'horizon of possibilities' rather than a single end point. Notions of formative assessment as directed towards 'closing the gap' between present understanding and the learning aimed for can be too restrictive if seen in this way, especially in subject areas that do not have a clear linear or hierarchical structure.

Peer- and self-assessment

The AfL practices described above emphasise changes in the teacher's role. However, they also imply changes in what pupils do and how they might become more involved in assessment and in reflecting on their own learning. Indeed, questioning, giving appropriate feedback and reflecting on criteria of quality can all be rolled up in peer- and self-assessment. This is what happened in a research study by Fontana and Fernandes (1994). Over a period of twenty weeks, primary school pupils were progressively trained to carry out self-assessment that involved setting their own learning objectives, constructing relevant problems to test their learning, selecting appropriate tasks, and carrying out self-assessments. Over the period of the experiment the learning gains of this group were twice as big as those of a matched 'control' group.

The importance of peer- and self-assessment was also illustrated by Frederiksen and White (1997) who compared learning gains of four classes taught by each of three teachers over the course of a term. All the classes had an evaluation activity each fortnight. The only thing that was varied was the focus of the evaluation. Two classes focused on what they liked and disliked about the topic; the other two classes focused on 'reflective assessment' which involved pupils in using criteria to assess their own work and to give one another feedback. The results were remarkable. All pupils in the 'reflective assessment group' made more progress than pupils in the 'likes and dislikes group'. However, the greatest gains were for pupils previously assessed as having weak basic skills. This suggests that low achievement in schools may have much less to do with a lack of innate ability than with pupils' lack of understanding of what they are meant to be doing and what counts as quality.

From 1999 to 2001 a development and research project was carried out by Paul Black and colleagues (2002, 2003), at King's College London with teachers in Oxfordshire and Medway (the King's, Medway and Oxfordshire Formative Assessment Project – KMOFAP), to test some of these findings in a British context because much of the earlier research came from other countries. They found peer-assessment to be an important complement to self-assessment because pupils learn to take on the roles of teachers and to see learning from their perspective. At the same time they can give and take criticism and advice in a non-threatening way, and in a language that children naturally use. Most importantly, as with self-assessment, peer-assessment is a strategy for 'placing the work in the hands of the pupils'.

Formative use of summative tests

The KMOFAP study was of 24 science and mathematics teachers in six secondary schools. In the second year, 12 English teachers also joined the project. The giving of regular tests was a familiar part of practice in these contexts, which some teachers were reluctant to relinquish. Attempts were therefore made to convert the practice to more formative purposes. Teachers took time to discuss test questions that gave particular difficulty and peer tutoring was used to tackle problems encountered by a minority. Thus teachers and pupils delved beneath the marks and grades to examine the evidence of learning, on which the summative judgements were based, and to find formative strategies for improvement. These researchers argue that although there is evidence of harmful effects of summative assessment on teaching, it is unrealistic to expect teachers and pupils to practise separation between assessment *of* learning and assessment *for* learning. So the challenge is to achieve a more positive relationship between the two.

Thoughtful and active learners

The ultimate goal of AfL is to involve pupils in their own assessment so that they can reflect on where they are in their own learning, understand where they need to go next and work out what steps to take to get there. The research literature sometimes refers to this as the processes of self-monitoring and self-regulation. It could also be a description of learning how to learn. In other words they need to understand both the desired *outcomes* of their learning and the *processes* of learning by which these outcomes are achieved, and they need to act on this understanding. They need to do this if they are to avoid the all-too-familiar experience of schooling which, as Mary Alice White noted in 1971, sometimes bears unfortunate similarities to ancient sea-faring: 'The daily chores, the demands, the inspections, become the reality, not the voyage, nor the destination.'

For learning how to learn to be effective, pupils need to become both thoughtful and active learners – they need to become autonomous. They must, in the end, take responsibility for their own learning; the teacher's role is to help them towards this goal. Assessment for learning is a vital tool for this purpose of promoting learning autonomy.

References

Note: Asterisked references are short booklets or leaflets designed for busy teachers to read.

*Assessment Reform Group (1999) *Assessment for Learning: beyond the black box.* University of Cambridge School of Education.

*Assessment Reform Group (2002a) *Assessment for Learning: 10 principles.* University of Cambridge Faculty of Education.

*Assessment Reform Group (2002b) *Testing, Motivation and Learning.* University of Cambridge Faculty of Education.

Black, P. and Wiliam, D. (1998a) Assessment and Classroom Learning, *Assessment in Education: Principles, Policy and Practice*, 5(1), pp. 5–75.

*Black, P. and Wiliam, D. (1998b) *Inside the Black Box: raising standards through classroom assessment.* King's College London, School of Education (now available from NFER/Nelson).

*Black, P., Harrison, C., Lee, C., Marshall, B. and Wiliam, D. (2002) *Working Inside the Black Box: assessment for learning in the classroom.* King's College London, Department of Education and Professional Studies (now available from NFER/Nelson).

Black, P., Harrison, C., Lee, C., Marshall, B. and Wiliam, D. (2003) *Assessment for Learning: putting it into practice.* Maidenhead, Open University Press.

Butler, R. (1988) Enhancing and Undermining Intrinsic Motivation: the effects of task-involving and ego-involving evaluation on interest and performance, *British Journal of Educational Psychology*, 58, pp. 1–14.

Crooks, T. (1988) The Impact of Classroom Evaluation Practices on Students, *Review of Educational Research*, 58, pp. 434–481.

Day, J. and Cordón, L (1993) Static and Dynamic Measures of Ability: an experimental comparison, *Journal of Educational Psychology*, 85, pp. 76–82.

Fontana, D. and Fernandes, M. (1994) Improvements in Mathematics Performance as a Consequence of Self-assessment in Portuguese Primary School Pupils, *British Journal of Educational Psychology*, 64, pp. 407–417.

Frederiksen, J. and White, B. (1997) Reflective Assessment of Students' Research Within an Inquiry-Based Middle School Science Curriculum. Paper presented at the Annual Meeting of the AERA, Chicago, IL.

Kluger, A. and DeNisi, A. (1996) The Effects of Feedback Interventions on Performance: a historical review, a meta-analysis, and a preliminary feedback intervention theory, *Psychological Bulletin*, 119, pp. 254–284.

*Millar, R. and Hames, V. (2003) *Towards Evidence-based Practice in Science Education 1: using diagnostic assessment to enhance learning.* Teaching and Learning Research Programme Research Briefing No. 1, University of Cambridge Faculty of Education.

Natriello, G. (1987) The Impact of Evaluation Processes on Students, *Educational Psychologist*, 22, pp. 155–175.

Sadler, D. R. (1989) Formative Assessment and the Design of Instructional Systems, *Instructional Science*, 18, pp. 119–144.

Vinner, S. (1997) From Intuition to Inhibition – mathematics education and other endangered species, in E. Pehkonen (ed.), *Proceedings of the 21st Conference of the International Group for the Psychology of Mathematics Education*, 1, pp. 63–78. Lahti, Finland: The University of Helsinki Lahti Research and Training Centre.

White, M. A. (1971) The View from the Pupil's Desk, in M. L. Silberman (ed.) *The Experience of Schooling.* New York, Holt, Rinehart and Winston.

Introducing the ideas and deciding a direction for development

Three kinds of materials are included here:

1 Presentation: learning how to learn through assessment for learning;
2 Audit and action-planning activity: planning for learning how to learn through assessment for learning;
3 Self-evaluation tool: staff questionnaire A: Classroom assessment practices and values.

The presentation (pages 15–18) can be used to introduce teachers to the key ideas underpinning assessment for learning as a way of helping pupils to learn how to learn. Changing accustomed practice is often challenging for teachers, so knowledge of the positive effects that AfL has been shown to have on learning and achievement can give teachers the confidence to take what they perceive to be risks. The second section of the presentation provides sets of very practical ideas for the development of classroom practice. The idea here is that teachers should be encouraged to select some to try out in their classrooms then feed back and discuss what they have learned with colleagues.

The presentation can be used as a way of initiating development in AfL with a group of teachers or as whole-school INSET. With breaks for discussion, this presentation will occupy a session of around one hour. You can find a PowerPoint version of this presentation at: http://www.learntolearn.ac.uk. The version on the website is accompanied with a notes page for each slide which indicates the points to focus upon.

The audit and action-planning activity (see page 19) is a follow-up to the presentation. It asks teachers to reflect on what they have heard and decide where they want to go next. It is a good idea to allow ten minutes or so for teachers to consider the activity as individuals before discussion and decision-making in groups. Departmental groups or key stage teams might be appropriate. Taken together the presentation and this action-planning activity might take a full morning or afternoon on a professional training day. Those leading these sessions will need to collect copies of the action plans so that school leaders can consider the best ways to co-ordinate and support development and monitor progress.

The alternative self-evaluation questionnaire (see pages 20–24) is best given to teachers to complete *before* a programme of professional development is fully planned because, in this context, it is intended to enable a form of needs analysis on which a programme can be built. Analysis of responses will alert INSET leaders or planning groups to practices that might need attention because, for example, they exhibit low practice levels or wide value-practice gaps. This may also assist decision-making about whether INSET should be school-wide or whether it should focus initially on supporting the development of specific groups of staff. Feedback of results from the questionnaire might be a useful part of whole-school or sub-group discussions.

Learning How to Learn

through assessment for learning

Learning in school

The analogy that might make the student's view more comprehensible to adults is to imagine oneself on a ship sailing across an unknown sea, to an unknown destination. An adult would be desperate to know where he [*sic*] is going. But a child only knows he is going to school . . . Very quickly, the daily life on board ship becomes all important . . . The daily chores, the demands, the inspections, become the reality, not the voyage, nor the destination.

(Mary Alice White, 1971)

Assessment for Learning (AfL)

Learners need to know:

- where they are in their learning
- where they are going
- how to get there.

Assessment for Learning is, essentially, concerned with helping students to develop these capabilities and involves learners and teachers seeking and interpreting evidence in order to help with this process.

Learning How to Learn (LHTL)

Learning how to learn is achieved when learners make sense of where they are in their learning, where they are going, and how to improve; in other words, when they engage in assessment for learning *for themselves.*

Developing learning autonomy is at the heart of LHTL

We use 'learning *how* to learn' rather than 'learning to learn' because the 'how' is important; it emphasises the *practices* that teachers and learners can employ to help pupils become more effective as learners.

What research says about AfL

Black and Wiliam (1998) undertook a review which built on earlier work by Natriello (1987) and Crooks (1988). 250 papers from education and psychology journals from 1987 to 1997 were reviewed and their finding reported in a special edition of the journal *Assessment in Education: Principles, Policy and Practice* (Volume 5, Issue 1) in 1998.

They also produced a short booklet entitled 'Inside the Black Box' for practitioners and policymakers, which sold about 50,000 copies in seven years.

Substantial effects

- Of the studies reviewed by Black and Wiliam, 50 provided quantitative evidence of the size of the gains that could be expected as a result of improving classroom assessment – an effect size of between 0.4 and 0.7 standard deviations.
- At school level an effect size of 0.7 would improve performance of secondary school students in GCSE by between one and two grades (and possibly three grades for the lowest attainers).
- An effect size of this magnitude locates AfL as being amongst the highest impact innovations in teaching and learning.

Black and Wiliam's three questions

- Is there evidence that improving the quality of assessment for learning in classrooms raises standards?
- Is there evidence that there is room for improvement in our current practice?
- Is there evidence about how to improve assessment for learning?

On the basis of the evidence from the 250 studies they reviewed, the answer to all three questions was 'yes'.

Key aspects of AfL

One way of thinking about AfL is to look at the key classroom activities that underpin it.

Some of these involve changes in teachers's practices:

- eliciting information about learning, especially through dialogue and questioning;
- providing appropriate feedback that helps learners know what to do to improve;
- ensuring learners can understand and judge quality through sharing criteria and exemplars.

Others are more concerned with changes in learners' practices:

- peer- and self-assessment, which can incorporate all three of the practices above.

Evidence: eliciting information

Vinner (1997) studied learners' responses to questions in the International Maths and Science Study. Some questions seemed to cause learners far more problems than apparently similar questions. For example, this question was answered correctly (a) by only 46% of children, with 39% choosing option (b).

Which fraction is the largest?   a) $\frac{4}{5}$, b) $\frac{3}{4}$, c) $\frac{5}{8}$, d) $\frac{7}{10}$

Many children develop the misconception that the largest fraction is that with the smallest denominator.

By asking questions, teachers try to establish whether students have understood what they are meant to be learning. If students answer the questions correctly, it is tempting to assume that the students' conceptions match those of the teacher. This is not always so; they may give the right answer for the wrong reason. 'Good' questions are those that encourage learners to make explicit their thinking, not just give 'right' answers.

Evidence: sharing criteria and self-assessment

Frederiksen and White (1997) undertook a study of three teachers, each of whom taught four parallel Y8 science classes in two US schools. In order to assess how representative was the sample, all the students in the study were given a basic skills test, and their scores were close to the national average.

Learners undertook seven two-week projects, each scored from 2 to 10. For a part of each week, two of each teacher's classes discussed their likes and dislikes about the teaching. The other two classes discussed how their work would be assessed and then self-assessed their work against criteria. All other teaching was the same. Mean scores for each group are shown below.

Group / Basic skills	Low	Medium	High
Likes and dislikes	4.6	5.9	6.6
Discussing criteria	6.7	7.2	7.4

Evidence: appropriate feedback

Butler (1988) investigated the effects of different kinds of feedback with 132 learners regarded as the most and least academically able in 12 classes. Teachers, curriculum and classroom context was kept the same; the only difference was the kind of written feedback provided to the learners (marks only, comments only, marks and comments).

For able learners, marks were a motivating factor; for less able, they were demotivating. There were no learning gains for pupils receiving marks only. Comment-only marking motivated both less and most able and gains were seen in learning achievement. However, giving marks alongside the comment completely negated the beneficial effects of the comments. Butler explains this by saying that marks are 'ego-involving' whereas comments, on their own, help learners focus on the task.

The use of both marks and comments is probably the most widespread form of feedback used in the United Kingdom, and yet this study (and other like it) show that it is no more effective than marks alone.

Practices: eliciting information

- Improving teacher questioning
  - closed v. open questions
  - low-order v. high-order questions
  - generating questions with colleague
- 'Hot seat' questioning
  - extended interaction with one student to scaffold learning
  - other students learn vicariously
- 'No hands up' (except to ask a question)
- Increased wait time
- Class poll to review current attitudes towards issue.

The most effective questions are those which necessitate reflection rather than recall. The 'best' questions may not be those which are 'discriminators' of levels of understanding, but rather those which stimulate reflection on the part of all learners.

A good question . . . can challenge and surprise, but should not be seen as a weapon by which to diminish others. A good question maintains student engagement, stimulates thought and evokes feelings.
(Morgan and Saxton, 1991)

Practices: sharing criteria

Learners benefit when they can locate current learning in relation to prior and future learning – 'where have we been?' as well as 'where are we going?'.

Learners need to come to an understanding of what counts as quality that is roughly similar to that possessed by their teachers (Sadler, 1989). However, teachers need also to be sensitive to creativity and achievement that goes beyond their expectations.

- Explaining learning objectives at start of lesson/unit and revisiting these throughout
- Criteria in students' language
- Posters of key words to talk about learning
  - e.g.: describe, explain, evaluate
- Planning/writing frames
- Annotated examples of different standards to 'flesh out' assessment criteria
- Opportunities for students to design their own tests.

Summary: what teachers need to do

- seek and interpret evidence of existing learning and performance (especially through questioning);
- provide feedback to help learners understand the strengths and weaknesses in their current learning, the standards aimed for, and how they might improve;
- provide opportunities for learners to improve their work;
- develop learners' own capacity to understand standards and to self-assess using criteria and exemplars;
- plan these elements as an integral part of their teaching.

Putting emphasis on these practices can require shifts in the way both teachers and pupils view their *roles* – it is not a trivial change but the results can be exciting.

Practices: appropriate feedback

Feedback in terms of marks, grades and levels is unlikely to improve learning, but feedback in terms of comments (whether written or oral) is.

But 'what kind of comments?' Any comment should cause thinking to take place. Moreover, feedback is only formative if it is actually used by the learner to improve. Thus, opportunities to work on improvement need to be provided.

- Comment-only marking
- Focused marking
- Explicit reference to criteria
- Suggestions on how to improve
  - 'strategy cards' ideas for improvement
  - 'scaffolding' rather than giving complete solutions
- Re-timing assessment: at the beginning or part way through a topic.

Practices: peer- and self-assessment

These strategies mesh with those on previous slides, but involve a shift in that learners are now centrally involved in asking questions, using criteria, exemplars and feedback to assess their own and others' work and identify ways forward.

Assessment need not be focussed on achievement measures, but can address levels of *confidence* with respect to 'threshold concepts' – either individually or collectively.

- Students assessing their own/peers' work
  - with marking schemes
  - with criteria
  - with exemplars
- Identifying group weaknesses
- Self-assessment of confidence and uncertainty
  - traffic lights
  - smiley faces
  - post-it notes
- End-of-lesson students' review.

Planning for learning how to learn through assessment for learning (audit and action-planning activity)

Individual, group or whole school

Audit

1   What do you do already?

Thinking about change

2   How could what you do already be improved?

3   What new practices could you introduce?

4   What old practices could you discard?

Planning for change

5   What do you plan to do?

6   Who will be involved?

7   What support/training/resources will you need?

8   What will be your timescale?

9   What milestones will you expect?

10. How will you evaluate success (methods/criteria)?

Name: _____ Role: _____

Staff questionnaire A: Classroom assessment practices and values (self-evaluation instrument)

Completing the questionnaire

1 Staff questionnaire A consists of 30 statements. Each statement relates to an aspect of assessment.

2 There are two scales for each of the 30 statements: scale X and scale Y. For each statement please tick one box only under scale X and one box only under scale Y.

3 You will notice in the example below that each statement appears in the centre, between scale X and scale Y.

4 Scale X on the left hand side is *about you*. Please read each statement and think about your own practices in relation to assessment. Tick the appropriate box to say how often or rarely you do each of the listed practices.

5 Scale Y on the right hand side asks you to indicate your educational values in relation to each of the listed practices. Irrespective of how much or how little of a practice you do, scale Y asks you to say how important you think the practice is for enhancing the quality of pupils' learning. Or, do you think the particular practice is simply bad practice? In this case you would tick the box in the fifth column in scale Y. Please tick only one box in scale X and one box in scale Y.

Example

	SCALE X Your assessment practices (About you)				Assessment practices		SCALE Y How important are assessment practices for creating opportunities for pupils to learn? (About your values)			
Never true	Rarely true	Often true	Mostly true			Not at all important	Of limited importance	Important	Crucial	Bad practice!
☐	✔	☐	☐		Parents are helped to think about how their child learns best.	☐	☐	☐	✔	☐

This respondent rarely helps parents to think about how their child learns best; however, even though this respondent only provides such guidance rarely, she thinks that such guidance is crucial for creating opportunities for pupils to learn.

Please turn over now and complete the questionnaire

SCALE Y

How important are assessment practices for creating opportunities for pupils to learn?

(About your values)

SCALE X

Your assessment practices

(About you)

Assessment practices

Not at all important	Of limited importance	Important	Crucial	Bad practice!	Assessment practices	Mostly true	Often true	Rarely true	Never true
☐	☐	☐	☐	☐	1. Assessment provides me with useful evidence of my pupils' understandings which I use to plan subsequent lessons.	☐	☐	☐	☐
☐	☐	☐	☐	☐	2. The next lesson I teach is determined more by the prescribed curriculum than by how well my pupils did in the last lesson.	☐	☐	☐	☐
☐	☐	☐	☐	☐	3. The main emphasis in my assessments is on whether my pupils know, understand or can do prescribed elements of the curriculum.	☐	☐	☐	☐
☐	☐	☐	☐	☐	4. The feedback that my pupils receive helps them improve.	☐	☐	☐	☐
☐	☐	☐	☐	☐	5. Pupils are told how well they have done in relation to others in the class.	☐	☐	☐	☐
☐	☐	☐	☐	☐	6. Pupils are given opportunities to decide their own learning objectives.	☐	☐	☐	☐
☐	☐	☐	☐	☐	7. I use questions mainly to elicit factual knowledge from my pupils.	☐	☐	☐	☐

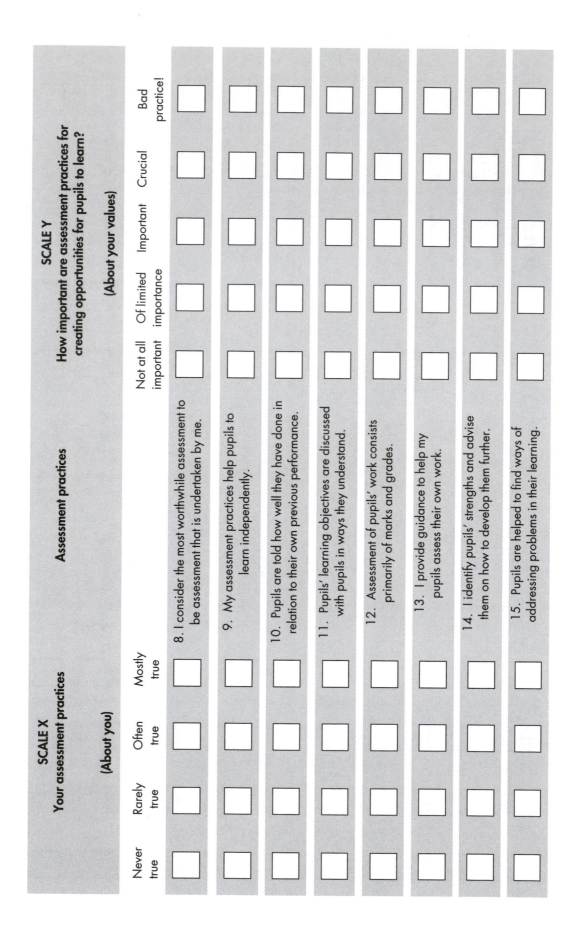

SCALE X
Your assessment practices
(About you)

SCALE Y
How important are assessment practices for creating opportunities for pupils to learn?
(About your values)

Never true	Rarely true	Often true	Mostly true	Assessment practices	Not at all important	Of limited importance	Important	Crucial	Bad practice!
☐	☐	☐	☐	8. I consider the most worthwhile assessment to be assessment that is undertaken by me.	☐	☐	☐	☐	☐
☐	☐	☐	☐	9. My assessment practices help pupils to learn independently.	☐	☐	☐	☐	☐
☐	☐	☐	☐	10. Pupils are told how well they have done in relation to their own previous performance.	☐	☐	☐	☐	☐
☐	☐	☐	☐	11. Pupils' learning objectives are discussed with pupils in ways they understand.	☐	☐	☐	☐	☐
☐	☐	☐	☐	12. Assessment of pupils' work consists primarily of marks and grades.	☐	☐	☐	☐	☐
☐	☐	☐	☐	13. I provide guidance to help my pupils assess their own work.	☐	☐	☐	☐	☐
☐	☐	☐	☐	14. I identify pupils' strengths and advise them on how to develop them further.	☐	☐	☐	☐	☐
☐	☐	☐	☐	15. Pupils are helped to find ways of addressing problems in their learning.	☐	☐	☐	☐	☐

SCALE X
Your assessment practices
(About you)

Assessment practices

SCALE Y
How important are assessment practices for creating opportunities for pupils to learn?
(About your values)

Never true	Rarely true	Often true	Mostly true	Assessment practices	Not at all important	Of limited importance	Important	Crucial	Bad practice!
☐	☐	☐	☐	16. Pupils are encouraged to view mistakes as valuable learning opportunities.	☐	☐	☐	☐	☐
☐	☐	☐	☐	17. Pupils are helped to think about how they learn best.	☐	☐	☐	☐	☐
☐	☐	☐	☐	18. I use questions mainly to elicit reasons and explanations from my pupils.	☐	☐	☐	☐	☐
☐	☐	☐	☐	19. I provide guidance to help pupils to assess one another's work.	☐	☐	☐	☐	☐
☐	☐	☐	☐	20. Pupils' errors are valued for what they reveal about how pupils are thinking.	☐	☐	☐	☐	☐
☐	☐	☐	☐	21. Pupils are helped to understand the learning purposes of each lesson or unit.	☐	☐	☐	☐	☐
☐	☐	☐	☐	22. Assessment of pupils' work is mainly in the form of comments.	☐	☐	☐	☐	☐
☐	☐	☐	☐	23. Pupils' learning objectives are determined mainly by the prescribed curriculum.	☐	☐	☐	☐	☐

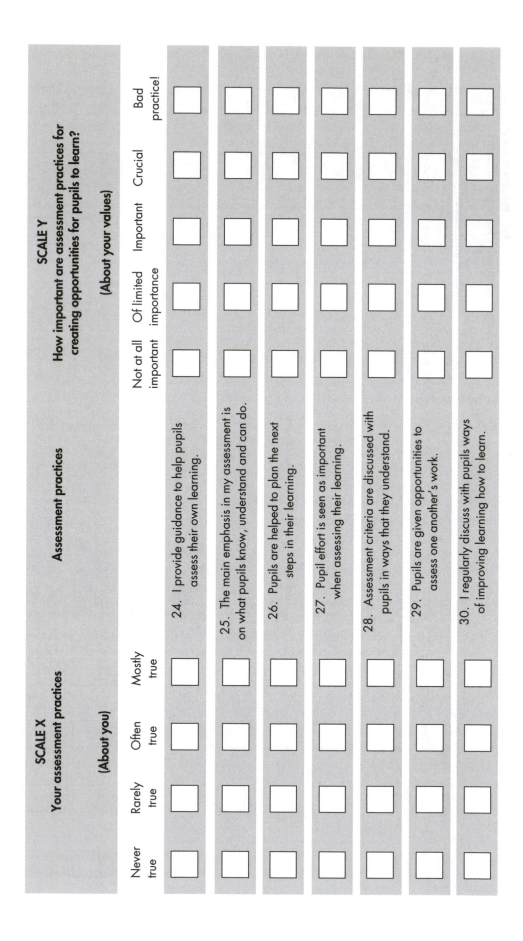

SCALE X
Your assessment practices
(About you)

Assessment practices

SCALE Y
How important are assessment practices for creating opportunities for pupils to learn?
(About your values)

Never true	Rarely true	Often true	Mostly true	Assessment practices	Not at all important	Of limited importance	Important	Crucial	Bad practice!
☐	☐	☐	☐	24. I provide guidance to help pupils assess their own learning.	☐	☐	☐	☐	☐
☐	☐	☐	☐	25. The main emphasis in my assessment is on what pupils know, understand and can do.	☐	☐	☐	☐	☐
☐	☐	☐	☐	26. Pupils are helped to plan the next steps in their learning.	☐	☐	☐	☐	☐
☐	☐	☐	☐	27. Pupil effort is seen as important when assessing their learning.	☐	☐	☐	☐	☐
☐	☐	☐	☐	28. Assessment criteria are discussed with pupils in ways that they understand.	☐	☐	☐	☐	☐
☐	☐	☐	☐	29. Pupils are given opportunities to assess one another's work.	☐	☐	☐	☐	☐
☐	☐	☐	☐	30. I regularly discuss with pupils ways of improving learning how to learn.	☐	☐	☐	☐	☐

Part II   Going deeper

Overview

This part contains a series of workshops that will help schools and teachers explore in more depth key classroom processes associated with assessment for learning and to support the development of practice.

The workshops are designed to be used by groups of teachers: either whole-school groups, departmental groups or groups drawn from different schools. In most workshops some materials – transcripts, excerpts, examples – are provided, but they all work best when teachers draw on their own experience and combine the ideas in the workshops with data from their own classrooms.

The workshops

Four of the workshops build on the four sets of practical strategies identified in the initial in-service session presented in Part I of this book:

- Workshop 1: Developing classroom talk through questioning
- Workshop 2: Feedback
- Workshop 3: Sharing criteria with learners
- Workshop 4: Peer- and self-assessment

A fifth workshop deals with what we know about how people learn. This was developed because teachers in other schools requested a workshop that would update their knowledge of learning theory. They realised that practical applications of theoretical ideas formed the basis of current practice or those they were attempting to develop. Better understanding of these ideas allowed them to appraise practice more critically and make well-founded judgements about directions for new development.

Duration and sequencing

Each workshop will take between 60 and 90 minutes with some follow-up work in classrooms. They are therefore suitable for either INSET days or after-school INSET sessions. They are 'freestanding', so they can be undertaken in any order and integrated into a school's development programme.

Links and resources

More detailed guides for facilitators, including additional notes on the research evidence, plus a downloadable guide for participants, can be found on the Learning How to Learn Project website at: http://www.learntolearn.ac.uk. The Association for Achievement and Improvement through Assessment (AAIA) also has a helpful website with downloadable resources. These can be found at: http://www.aaia.org.uk/assessment.htm.

How schools have used the workshop resources

Some schools worked systematically through all the workshops over a period of time with space between to implement and evaluate new practices.

Primary school co-ordinator

I was able to talk with my Senior Management Team, my Key Stage Co-ordinators and then say, 'Look, we've got this workshop coming up, what do we think are the real issues that need to be covered?' and then, following it, 'Do we think that the real issues were covered? What are our action points?' and then the feedback process.

Others selected particular workshops according to identified needs.

Secondary school co-ordinator

There was already workshop materials for feedback, so I think [we chose] one of the other strategies. Staff here had identified the questioning as an area they had wanted to develop – in the September training day. What happened afterwards was that the departments went away and we did workshops with them. My co-leaders did a workshop for their team. Even with the wealth of other stuff like literacy, numeracy, skills development and so on, AfL should become part of the natural working of the school. It ought to become part of departmental practice. What we are hoping is that it will become much more part of their everyday teaching practice.

Another school made a special request for a workshop on learning theory to get them started.

Infants school co-ordinator

We planned how we were going to do them. The first one was the theories of learning, and I think the second two were peer- and self-evaluation and feedback. We did change the order slightly as we went along; we didn't stick to the original order. I think the key decision was allowing time for practice, for a change, for the change in practice to happen. We wanted to take each workshop, make sure that some change happened as a result of that practice, and discuss that in order that it becomes part of your everyday working. I think it's generated a lot of new ideas, reading, a lot of evaluation of practice, and failure. I think people were more willing to take risks, try new ideas and say 'That didn't work', and be much more open about that. After an input from a workshop, we then decide what we're going to do on our own, and what we're going to do as a school. The workshops started the whole process off. [Also] meeting with other schools and sharing ideas as part of a whole was key – so that we weren't in isolation.

Materials

Each of the workshops has the following structure:

- aims
- evidence from research
- workshop tasks
- task materials.

Workshops 1 to 4 also have comments, drawn from school project logs; these provide illustrations or evaluations of how schools have used the workshop. All of these sections can be photocopied for workshop participants to use. Alternatively, separate Facilitator's and Participant's Guides, some with more detail, can be downloaded from the project website.

Running the workshops

At the beginning of each workshop it is a good idea to spend about ten minutes looking again at parts of the initial INSET presentation connected with the workshop topic and expanding on these with ideas from the 'Evidence from research' section. The workshop tasks can then be carried out. In most cases, there is a short activity to stimulate critical reflection, followed by one or more activities to help teachers plan to develop their own practice. These need follow-through in classroom contexts, and later opportunities to discuss and evaluate teachers' experiences, with a view to further development.

Workshop 1: Developing classroom talk through questioning

Aims

After completing this workshop, teachers should be able to:
1 understand the principles for effective classroom talk, especially questioning;
2 plan, introduce, and then evaluate, some new questioning practices in lessons.

Evidence from research

1 The most common reasons given by teachers for using questioning (Brown and Wragg, 1993) are, in order of perceived importance:
   a encouraging thought, understanding of ideas, phenomena, procedures and values;
   b checking understanding, knowledge and skills;

    c   gaining attention to task, warming-up, moving towards a specific teaching point;

    d   review, revision, recall, reinforcement.

2 In practice, most teachers' questions to pupils are concerned with factual recall. A relatively small proportion of questions encourage and develop thinking skills. This would suggest a gap between the priorities expressed in 1, above, and prevailing classroom practice.

3 Most pupils are dependent upon their teacher to see the 'big picture' of the course or lesson and need constant 'signposting' to help them see how specific elements and tasks fit into this. Questioning is a way of focusing direction and purpose as well as monitoring pupil understanding.

4 Pupils find oral feedback more effective than written. Questioning can be considered as one important form of oral feedback in which pupils are involved in a 'managed' dialogue with the teacher.

5 A good question should have reason, focus, clarity and appropriate intonation. It can challenge and surprise, but should not be seen as a weapon by which to diminish others. A good question maintains student engagement, stimulates thought and evokes feelings (Morgan and Saxton, 1991).

6 Good responses are achieved primarily through active listening and allowing quality thinking time in tune with the social context of the classroom as well as the particular subject content. Increased wait time is needed in most teachers' questioning in order to encourage more thoughtful responses. This can be achieved by building a relationship of trust between teacher and class and through various group strategies.

7 Some of the most common errors in teachers' questioning are:
- asking too many questions at once;
- asking a question and answering it yourself;
- asking questions only to the brightest or most likeable;
- asking a difficult question too early;
- asking irrelevant questions;
- always asking the same type of question;
- asking questions in a threatening way;
- not indicating a change in the type of question;
- not using probing answers;
- not giving pupils time to think;
- failing to see the implications of answers;
- failing to build on answers.

8 Questioning strategies can be planned by identifying lead questions, ideally in conjunction with colleagues, and trying to anticipate the range of potential responses.

9 Planning needs to be complemented by teacher skills in: structuring; pitching and clarity; direction and distribution; pausing and pacing; prompting and probing; listening and responding; and sequencing of the questioning.

10 Teachers need to shift the balance of their questioning from lower-order questions (knowledge, comprehension, application) towards more higher-order questions (analysis, synthesis, evaluation).

11 This can be achieved through extended interaction with one student and 'scaffolding' learning such that others in the group or class learn vicariously.

12 Once the expectations of questioning have been established by the teacher, pupils will have a greater tendency to develop their own questions and engage in active classroom dialogue and a deeper level of learning.

References

Brown, G. and Wragg, E. (1993) *Questioning*, London, Routledge.
Morgan, N. and Saxton, J. (1991) *Teaching Questioning and Learning*, London, Routledge.

Workshop tasks

This workshop consists of two tasks and a follow-up task:

Task 1: analysing practice and developing principles (about one hour)

1   Read 'A Tale of Two Lessons' (see 'Task materials' below).
2   In groups of four, allocate two colleagues to focus on Teacher A and two colleagues to focus on Teacher B.
3   In these pairs: list the characteristics of (a) the teacher's talk/questions, (b) pupils' talk/responses.
4   Compare lists in the group of four.
5   Construct a typology which describes the differences between these two teaching styles.
6   Look at the 'Evidence from research' to see if there is evidence that one style is more effective than the other for pupils' learning.
7   Now generate some principles for effective classroom talk/questioning.
8   Discuss whether these are likely to be transferable to your subject(s) and the age range you teach.

Task 2: planning questioning (about 20 minutes)

In pairs, plan a lesson with questioning particularly in mind. Think about:

1   lead questions;
2   follow-on questions;
3   contingent teaching, i.e. what you will do next when pupils respond in particular ways that you might anticipate.

Follow-up task: developing practice

In the same pairs as Task 2:

1   Arrange to observe one another teaching the lesson you planned in Task 2 using your principles (Task 1) as a framework for analysis. Recording on audio- or video-tape will assist later discussion.
2   Arrange to meet to discuss feedback and do some more planning:
   •   describe what you saw;
   •   discuss what you both learnt;
   •   decide what you will do next.

Task materials

A Tale of Two Lessons

Source: Goldsworthy, A. (2000) *Raising Attainment in Primary Science*, GHPD, Reed Educational and Professional Publishing Ltd. Reproduced here with permission.

Two Year 4 classes are having a science lesson on dissolving. In their previous lesson, both classes mixed a variety of solids and liquids together and the teacher asked the children to observe what happened. Both teachers have written detailed plans with the following clear learning objective: 'Children should learn that some solids dissolve in water and that although the solid cannot be seen, it is still present.' Both teachers have good classroom control and both have sufficient good quality equipment readily available. Their lessons proceed as follows.

TEACHER A

Teacher: Right. Watch me as I show you what I want you to do today for science. Here is a beaker. I'm going to put in some water to about half way. I've got some salt here. I'm going to add a spoonful of salt to the water and stir it. Before I do that, tell me – is salt a solid or a liquid?

Two pupils wave their hands in the air and teacher nods in the direction of one of them.

Pupil W: A solid.
Teacher: Good. So I'm going to add this solid salt to the water. Is water a solid or a liquid?

Ten pupils put their hands up. Teacher picks one of the lower achieving pupils to answer.

Pupil X: A solid.
Teacher: Is it?
Pupil W: No, it's a liquid.
Teacher: That's right. So I add this solid salt to this liquid water and stir. Look the salt has mixed in with the water. You can't see it any more, but it's still there. We can use another sense to make sure of that – we could taste it. Salty water isn't harmful so we can taste it safely.

Teacher dips finger in solution and tastes it.

Teacher: Ugh! Salty. Now, when a solid mixes in with a liquid like this, so you can't see it any more, we say it has dissolved. And we call the mixture a solution. What I want you to do today is to mix some different solids with water to see if they dissolve. You will try three different solids, sugar, flour and sand.

Teacher organises the class into groups. Pupils collect equipment and work through the task, recording their results by putting a tick or a cross against the name of each solid to show whether it has dissolved or not. Teacher goes round to each group to make sure they are following the instructions and keeping to the task.

Teacher: OK. You've all finished. What did you find out? Did the sand dissolve and form a solution with the water?

Pupils all wave hands in the air. Teacher selects one to answer.

Pupil Y: No.
Teacher: Good. And what about the sugar?

Pupils all wave hands in the air again. Teacher selects one to answer.

Pupil Z: It dissolved.
Teacher: Right. And the flour?

Pupils all wave hands in the air. Teacher selects Pupil X to answer.

Pupil X: Yes.
Teacher: Are you sure? Did it dissolve?
Pupil X: No.
Teacher: No, it didn't. So the only solid that dissolved in the water and made a solution was the sugar. Check that you've all got a tick by sugar. Neither the flour nor the sand dissolved. Check that you put a cross by them. Change it if you need to. Well that was pretty straight-forward wasn't it? Well done. You've worked well today. Now clear away your equipment and you can go out to play.

TEACHER B

Teacher: Right. In our last science lesson we mixed some different materials together and described what happened. Some of you used this word.

Teacher writes 'dissolving' on the board.

Teacher: I've looked at your work and some of you seemed to be using the word dissolving in different ways. What we are going to do today is think about what we mean by dissolving. At the end of this lesson I will be looking for children who have a very clear idea of how we know when something has dissolved. OK. The first thing I want you to do is to imagine that a friendly alien has just landed on Earth and wants you to explain what dissolving means. Remember that the alien knows nothing about it. Work with your partner and decide what you would say. You have three minutes. Go.

Teacher does not interfere with pupils while they are talking in pairs.

Teacher: Right – I'd like to hear your ideas. Let's start with you two.

Teacher indicates a pair of pupils.

Pupil M: We thought that when something dissolves it disappears.
Teacher: Thanks, I'll write that on the board. Let's see if there are any other ideas.

Teacher indicates another pair of pupils.

Pupil N: We said that you have to mix things up to make them dissolve.
Teacher: So you're saying that dissolving is mixing things up. Have I got that right?
Pupil N: Yes, that's what we thought anyway.
Teacher: OK. That's another idea. I'll write that down.

Teacher continues taking in a few more ideas and writing them on the board.

Teacher: Thanks for that. You've come up with lots of ideas about the word dissolving. We'll look at our ideas again at the end of the lesson and see whether we still agree with them. Right, now what I want you to do is to try mixing three different solids – sugar, sand and flour – with some water. Get three beakers of water and add in a spoonful of each substance and stir them. While you do it, I want you to think about these three things:

Teacher writes these three questions on the board.

1   *What do the three materials look like before you mix them with the water?*
2   *Can something still be there, even if you can't see it?*
3   *What do you think the mixtures would look like if you left them to stand for a day?*

Teacher: You will be doing the practical work in groups. Each group needs to write out the three questions, so you can make quick notes beside them while you're doing the practical work. Try to make note of everyone's ideas. I will come round and see what you have said.

Teacher moves among the groups referring to the three questions and challenging pupils to respond.

Teacher: OK. You've all finished. Let's look at your ideas.

Teacher takes in ideas and, with reference to previous work done with the class, establishes that all the materials they added to the water are solids.

Teacher: What about the second question? Can something be there even if we can't see it? What did you think about that one?

Teacher indicates a pair of pupils.

Pupil P: We thought about other things that we know are there but we can't see them, like air.
Pupil Q: Yes. We thought that when the sugar mixes in, it might still be there in the water but we can't see it.
Teacher: OK – so you think the sugar is still there, even though we can't see it. Could you put your hand up if you agree with that?

Most pupils put hands in the air.

Teacher: Some of you didn't agree. Can I ask you (indicates pupil) to tell us why?
Pupil R: Yes. We weren't sure.
Pupil S: Part of me wants to say the sugar's still there, but another part of me says it can't be there if I can't see it.
Teacher: Um – yes it's hard isn't it? If you just use your eyes, it looks as if the sugar has disappeared. I wonder if it's worth thinking about other senses we could use to find out if the sugar's still there.
Pupils R
and S: Oh – yeah! We could taste it.
Teacher: Right – good thinking. Sugar and water are safe to taste so will you two come and taste it.

Pupils taste sugar solution and declare it to be sweet.

Teacher: So we seem to be saying that the sugar is there because we can taste it, even though we can't see it. Now what about that last question? What do you think these mixtures will look like after one day? I know you've made some notes. Can you draw three quick sketches to show me what you think they'll look like?

Teacher quickly walks round the class, seeing what is being drawn.

Teacher: OK. Most of you seem to think the sugar and water and the sand and water mixtures will look the same as they do now. I've got some here that I mixed up yesterday. Let's see if you're right.

Teacher produces prepared mixtures.

Teacher: Looks like you're right. Now when it came to thinking about the flour and water mixture, you drew different pictures. Some of you thought it would stay as a cloudy mixture and some of you thought it would separate out. Let's see what happened.

Teacher produces a flour water mixture, which has separated out.

Teacher: So the flour and water didn't stay mixed. Now, you've got two minutes to think about which of the three solid materials dissolved in the water and how we can tell when something has dissolved.

Teacher collects in responses and class works together to produce the following definition of dissolving for the visiting alien, 'Dissolving is when a solid mixes with a liquid so that you can't see any solid bits anymore. Even though you can't see the solid stuff, it is still there. When something has dissolved it stays mixed and doesn't separate out.' Class agrees that only sugar has dissolved. They compare this to their original ideas.

Teacher: Turn to your partners and tell them something you've learnt about dissolving today.

Teacher collects in a couple of responses.

Teacher: So do you think we've got a better idea of what we mean by dissolving?
Pupils: Yes.
Teacher: Scientists have to think hard about the words they use and what they mean, and today you've done just that. Well done. You've worked hard. Now clear away your equipment and you can go out to play.

How schools have used this workshop

The examples below illustrate how one school adapted the follow-up observation task, and how another school adapted ideas from the popular television programme *Who Wants to be a Millionaire?* to develop questioning techniques.

Primary school

The staff conducted an audit of questioning practice using Teaching Assistants (TAs) as observers. Teachers provided feedback on this. It was their view that TAs are now aware of the issues about questioning although they were a little apprehensive about the observation task at first – they initially saw it as asking them to 'spy' on teachers. A clear difference was observed across subjects: questions were more open in literacy, and there was more 'scaffolding' by teachers in this context. There was little evidence of this in numeracy. Teachers commented that they thought they allowed more open discussion with children they considered more able and tended to give more structure to those who struggle. They began to question the wisdom of this.

Secondary school teacher

'Phone a friend' and 'No hands up' were introduced as questioning techniques with my Year 11 group. 'No hands up' can be useful in most lessons but I find 'phone a friend' is useful to recap a chunk of work. With Year 11, we recapped three lessons of work using the above strategies. I initially picked on a pupil to answer a question; they then nominated the next person and so on. If they didn't know the answer then they 'asked a friend' who is more likely to know the answer. By the end of the lesson all pupils had answered two questions each. It was a valuable lesson and all students were engaged in listening to questions and answers. Also, all pupils had to participate in the lesson.

Workshop 2: Feedback

Aims

After completing this workshop, teachers should:

- understand how effective feedback helps pupils to understand their strengths and weaknesses and improve their learning;
- be able to create formative feedback on pupils' work that will improve their learning;
- be able to plan to implement effective feedback practices.

Evidence from research

1 Feedback can be oral or written. There is no unequivocal evidence that one is better than the other; it depends on context.
2 More effective teachers use praise rather less often than less effective teachers.
3 Praise needs to be specific, describing what is praiseworthy, rather than generalised.
4 Feedback is more effective if it focuses on the task (task-involving) rather than the person (ego-involving).
5 Grades, marks, scores, ticks, etc. have little effect on subsequent performance.
6 Frequent feedback on behaviour and presentation (e.g. neatness) impairs its meaning as feedback on quality of thinking.
7 Narrative comments help pupils to understand how to improve.
8 Indications of areas for improvement and possible strategies are better than total solutions (e.g. teachers' corrections of work) because pupils have to think.
9 Opportunities need to be provided for pupils to improve on earlier efforts.
10 There are dangers in making public feedback that is related to individuals, but public feedback involving the whole class in general discussion is valuable.
11 Mistakes can be viewed as important learning opportunities.
12 If pupils' efforts are recognised they are more likely to believe they can improve. If they think success depends on innate ability they may give up in order to avoid failure.

References

Bangert-Drowns, R.L., *et al.* (1991) The instructional effect of feedback in test-like events, *Review of Educational Research*, 85, pp. 213–238.

Butler, R. (1987) Task-involving and ego-involving properties of evaluation: effects of different feedback conditions on motivational perceptions, interest and performance, *Journal of Educational Psychology*, 79, pp. 474–482.

Dweck, C. (1986) Motivational processes affecting learning, *American Psychologist*, 41, pp. 1,040–1,048.

Kluger, A. and DeNisi, A. (1996) The effects of feedback interventions on performance: a historical review, a meta-analysis and a preliminary feedback intervention theory, *Psychological Bulletin*, 119, pp. 254–284.

Tunstall, P. and Gipps, C. (1996) Teacher feedback to young children in formative assessment: a typology, *British Educational Research Journal*, 22, pp. 389–404.

Workshop tasks

This workshop consists of a pre-workshop task, three tasks and a follow-up task.

Pre-workshop task

Each workshop participant should collect and bring to the workshop four copies of one piece of unmarked work of one pupil (or some kind of representation – photograph, audio-tape, video-tape – if it is an artefact or performance).

Task 1: examining marking practice (about 10 minutes)

1   Look at the list of comments collected over one year from one pupil's work across a range of subjects (see 'Task materials' below).
2   With a colleague make a list of your reactions. Discuss whether the pupil will get a sense of their strengths and weaknesses and what he or she needs to do to improve.

Task 2: developing practice (about 25 minutes)

1   In groups of four, or fewer, examine the pieces of unmarked work brought to the session. Discuss the following questions:
   • What is worth commenting on?
   • What is not worth commenting on?
   • What are the strengths?
   • What are the weaknesses? Do these matter?
   • What is the source of weakness? How do you/can you know?
   • How can the work be improved?
2   Individually:
   • Compose what you will write on the pupil's work (or what you will say to them);
   • Decide what record you will keep of this.

Task 3: creating principles and a plan for action (about 15 minutes)

Whole group:
- Based on your discussions in Task 2, create a set of principles and procedures for marking.
- Plan implementation with targets and timescale.
- Consider how to communicate changes to pupils, parents, inspectors.

Follow-up task: implementing and reviewing action

- Implement over the next half term or so.
- Review and amend in consultation with others in your group.

Task materials

Marking practice: transcriptions of examples from a Year 7 pupil's work, 2003/4

SUBJECT A

- Excellent effort, A1 merit
- Nice
- Well organised
- Superb, A1 merit
- Excellent, A1 merit
- A1
- Good try, A1
- A1 merit
- Not all of them
- Excellent work
- A1 merit
- A1 merit, Excellent idea
- Colour?
- Fantastic detail, A1 merit
- Well done you have shown clear understanding
- Keep up the excellent c/w
- Excellent
- Wonderful piece, great adverts, Merit
- Excellent presentation
- Excellent general c/w!

SUBJECT B

- 3 × Sp (corrected), yes a well written letter
- Marginal comments: Careful with verb tenses 3 × Sp (corrected), ticks and '?'
- Yes a very good effort with lots of good pictures – more care with spelling please
- This is a really nice map – well presented. Good Work
- Marginal comments – section bracketed – 'what?' Sp × 2 (corrected in text) – adds an 'and', changes 'he'd' to 'he had', crossings out 'of' and 'there';

- Generally well written but it takes a while to get anywhere! Some confusion in places.
[change to a supply teacher]
- These are good drawings and you've remembered the quotes well done
- 10/10, 8/8, 10/10
- Wow!
- Brilliant (stamped)
- Brilliant (stamped)

SUBJECT C

- Well done, A1
- Good
- Good
- Right answer written in next to error
- Good
- Good work H!
- Use only – impossible/possible/certain (corrected using these terms) – A1 very good effort, one merit
- Super effort, A1
- V.Good + errors corrected
- V.gd well done
- Excellent

SUBJECT D

- Run gas down (correction)
- A2
- A2 Good clear answers, Well done
- A good effort but slightly confusing B2
- Marginal note – strongest
- 10/10 + smiley face
- Marginal note – lower case, one word; Sp × 2; Good B2
- Good use of diagrams
- A3 A good try A2 – come and see me if you don't understand
- A1 fantastic Merit
- A2 Some good points
- Fill this in (arrow pointing spot)
- These arrows should be going the same way as the compass
- Good observations
- Good So what does this tell you about an electro magnet – compare to bar magnet
- B2
- C3 You have done some good work, but you need to be consistent. I think you are capable of A1 grades. Target – include hypothesis and conclusions for every practical

SUBJECT E

- A1 Colourful! Answer in full sentences
- A1 A good effort
- A1 Good
- Colour these figures
- A1 Good effort

- Label this figure
- Good
- Good effort
- A1, Good effort
- Don't begin sentences with because

SUBJECT F

- A1 Muy Bien
- A2 Sp × 1 corrected, Learn (upside down question mark)
- A2 Buen esfuerzo
- Buen trabajo – (sticker)
- A2 Bien
- A1 Bien (unreadable), Sp × 1 corrected 20 = veinte
- A1 Bravo
- B3 No has terminado – incompleto
- A4 Mira las correciones
- A2 Estupendo
- A1 Bien hecho
- B2 Muy Bien un/una
- B2 Aprende – Dinamarca, Gran Bretaña
- Sp × 4
- B2 Presantación por favor
- A1 Bien merito
- A2 See detail e.g. accents
- A1 Bien esfuerzo. Keep an eye on feminine adjectives
- 1 error, Muy bien
- ! Muy Bien!
- B3
- A1 Excellente
- A1 Muy Bien

SUBJECT G

- B3 H, look through this list again. Some are opinions not fact
- Not a full sentence
- B2/3 Some interesting information
- Marginal comment – good. Sp × 1 + Gr × 1 both corrected. A1 This is an excellent evaluation H!
- A2
- A2

How schools have used this workshop

School co-ordinators commented on both use and value:

Primary school

The feedback workshop will give opportunity for staff to reflect on their current practice as well as identifying the ways of giving feedback that we want to trial as a whole school. [Later] Each year group fed back their experiences of working on new feedback strategies. Photocopied examples of feedback were shown to the whole staff. Staff felt the new strategies were beneficial and would continue working on them. The school assessment working party will meet to pull together some of the staff experiences with a view to adapting the current school marking policy.

Infants' school

The feedback tied in with our marking policy, plus our OfSTED criteria. So I think that was very high on the agenda, because it was something that we were working on anyway. It was interesting that staff found it more difficult to give feedback if the learning objective was not known, thus reinforcing the workshop.

Secondary school

And what's already emerged as being very clear is that a 'no grades' approach and 'comments only' feedback has been very, very successful and effective. And so we already know what the message is going to be. And then we thought of things like, well how do we get kids to understand what is a good structure for feeding back. Well, let's have them assessing each other.

Workshop 3: Sharing criteria with learners

Aims

After completing this workshop, teachers should:

- understand some reasons why pupils may produce different responses to the same prompts;
- be able to create a scheme for organising the sharing of criteria with learners and using it in the classroom;
- be able to plan for the implementation of these strategies.

Evidence from research

1   To many pupils, school appears to be a series of activities that make little sense. They spend their time negotiating their way through these tasks with as little damage as possible to their self-esteem. They end up 'doing school' or 'doing stuff'.

2   Pupils' work becomes more purposeful if they have access to the 'chart' that helps them see that they are 'getting somewhere' in their learning. Royce Sadler (1989, p. 121) notes:

> The indispensable conditions for improvement are that the student comes to hold a concept of quality roughly similar to that held by the teacher, is continuously able to monitor the quality of what is being produced during the act of production itself, and has a repertoire of alternative moves or strategies from which to draw at any given point.

3   For some activities, such as 'being able to subtract one three-digit number from another', it is relatively straightforward for a pupil to know whether they have achieved this or not. For other aims of learning, such as 'writing a good story', there cannot be any hard-and-fast criteria for success, but pupils can be helped to develop what Guy Claxton calls 'a nose for quality'.

4   Pupils often hold quite different views of quality from the teacher. There is evidence that middle-class pupils are more likely to produce responses that accord with the teacher's expectations. Barry Cooper and Máiréad Dunne found that working-class pupils were more likely to introduce ideas from their own experiences into their responses than middle-class pupils, who were more likely to realise when this was not relevant.

5   Differences between other groups of pupils, for example, boys and girls, or children from different ethic or cultural groups, can be explained in similar ways.

6   Pupils improve their learning and attainment when they have opportunities to think about what counts as good work. However, much more significantly, the improvements appear to be greater for pupils with weak basic skills. This suggests that, at least in part, low achievement in schools is exacerbated by pupils not understanding what it is they are meant to be learning.

7   Understanding the criteria themselves is only the starting point. At the beginning, the words do not have the meaning for the pupil that they have for the teacher. Just giving 'quality criteria' or 'success criteria' to pupils will not work, unless pupils have a chance to see what this might mean in the context of their own work. One strategy is to use examples of pupils' work to show pupils what criteria look like in practice. These do not have to be 'exemplary' in the sense that they are examples of very good work. Pupils often learn best from seeing work that is just a little better than the standard they currently achieve.

References

Claxton, G. (1995). What kind of learning does self-assessment drive? Developing a 'nose' for quality: comments on Klenowski, *Assessment in Education: principles, policy and practice*, 2(3), pp. 339–343.

Cooper, B. and Dunne, M. (1999). *Assessing children's mathematical knowledge: social class, sex and problem-solving*. Buckingham, Open University Press.

Frederiksen, J. and White, B. (1997). Reflective assessment of pupils' research within an inquiry-based middle school science curriculum. In *Proceedings of the Annual Meeting of the AERA Conference*, Chicago, IL.

Murphy, P. and Elwood. J. (1998). Gendered experiences, choices and achievement – exploring the links, *International Journal of Inclusive Education*, 2(2), pp. 95–118.

Sadler, D. R. (1989). Formative assessment and the design of instructional systems, *Instructional Science*, 18, 119–144.

Workshop tasks

This workshop consists of a pre-workshop task and three tasks. An alternative task to Task 2 is provided; this is suitable for teachers who are 'further down this road'.

Pre-workshop task

Workshop participants should collect and bring to the workshop a small range of pupils' work. Ideally this should be unmarked but should represent a spread from strong to weak responses to a task. One set of such work will be sufficient for a group of four participants.

Task 1: boys' and girls' responses (about 10 minutes)

In an English language survey, 15-year-old pupils were asked to look at two pictures of demoiselle flies and 'describe' them, paying particular attention to those differences that were 'most important for telling them apart'. As it was an assessment activity, teachers did not explain beforehand precisely what they wanted the pupils to do. Pupils had to work this out themselves from the wording of the instruction.

1   Read the two highly rated responses made to the task on the demoiselle fly (see 'Task materials' below). One is from a boy and one is from a girl.
2   After you have read the two responses, decide which was written by the boy and which was written by the girl (this shouldn't take long!) and then, in pairs, discuss why you think the two pupils produced such different responses to the same task.
3   Discuss your ideas with the rest of the group.

Task 2: creating a scheme for sharing criteria with learners (about 40 minutes)

The idea behind this task is that you provide pupils with a range of responses to a task, graduated from weak to good. It was stimulated by the work of a history teacher who would typically give pupils a source document, a question relating to the document, and four different responses, which the pupils had to rank in order of quality. They would then be asked to discuss the basis of their judgements.

1   In groups of three or four, look at the range of task responses brought to the workshop and, in the first instance, rank them in order of quality. (Avoid making direct reference to prescribed national curriculum criteria at this point, in order to come to a personal judgement.) As far as possible, try to ensure that these pieces of work are not ranked on surface criteria (e.g. length of response, sophistication of words used, neatness or spelling).

2   In your group, try to determine what it is that makes the better pieces of work better than the others – these judgements may now take account of national curriculum criteria but they should also take account of more task specific criteria or unanticipated aspects of the response. These ideas might be written down on an annotation sheet and attached to each piece of work in preparation for building a bank of exemplars.

3   In the whole group, discuss your views and reactions to the workshop task.

Task 3: planning for action (about 10 minutes)

In the whole group, discuss the strengths and limitations of this kind of 'scheme' for sharing criteria with learners and how you could use it in the classroom.

Alternative task

The Learning How to Learn Project has identified a number of practical strategies developed by schools for sharing criteria:

- explaining learning objectives at start of lesson/unit;
- translating criteria into pupils' language;
- designing posters, or flash cards, of key words to use in talk about learning – these may be subject specific or they may be generic words that are interpreted differently in different contexts, e.g. describe, explain, evaluate;
- devising planning/writing frames to help pupils to structure their work;
- developing a bank of annotated examples of different standards to 'flesh out' assessment criteria;
- providing opportunities for pupils to design their own tests/tasks.

Discuss which of these are already used in your school or department, and which you wish to develop further. At a subsequent meeting participants could describe and evaluate their experiences of using these activities.

Task materials

The Demoiselle Fly

From: White, J. (1988) *The Language of Science: science report for teachers: 11.* Assessment of Performance Unit. London, Department of Education and Science/Welsh Office. Reproduced here with permission.

RESPONSE 1 (EXACT TRANSCRIPTION)

The demoiselle fly in general has a short thorax long abdomen and bulbous compound eyes.

   Type A has all the aforementioned qualities but differs from type B in the following ways:

1   It has six long black legs with long hairs on top and lower parts of its leg's. Type B only has four leg's and has hair's on the bottom of its forelegs and top of its hindlegs only.

2   Type A has opaque wing's which are short and wide. Type B has transparent wings which are noteably longer and thinner than type A's.

3   Type A has its abdomen segmented into fairly small parts, the end section tapering to a point. Type B has it's abdomen made up of fairly small parts the end part tapering downwards to make it triangular.

4   The most notable difference between the two is their markings. Type A is Brown and green on it's thorax, having brown wing's which get lighter towards the edges and a brown abdomen. Type B is light blue and light brown on its thorax having colourless wing's apart from 3 brown spots on the end of it's wings and a blue brown and black abdomen with just a tinge of pink all over it.

5   Type A's eyes are brown, and bisected latterally with a jagged line. Type B's are blue (pale) with a black spot in the centre.

6   Type A has pointed mandibles but type B's is box shaped.

RESPONSE 2 (EXACT TRANSCRIPTION)

It is one of those lazy hot days in summer when everything is warm and very quiet. The trees surrounding the lake at the bottom of the hill are swaying silently and the ripples on the lake give the impression of peace and tranquillity.

At the end of the lake are reeds and lilies. Flies buzz dozily among the tall grasses, look for food. Bees laze among the pollen filled lilies, drinking their sweet nectar and the demoiselle flies perch motionless on the tall green fronds of the reids.

There are two in particular, one male, one female, that catch my eye as I lie against the sturdy trunk of an ancient oak. They are the most beautiful creatures I have ever seen, but they are both different.

One has lacy wings, so clear I can see the water's edge through them. Its colouring is of brilliant pinks and blues, and it stands out amongst the yellow buttercups that surround it. Its abdomen is long, like a finger, and incredibly thin. It looks so fragile, as though any sudden movement may snap it, like a twig. Its lacy wings stretch back, almost to the full length of the abdomen, like delicate fans, cooling it body. Its head is small but bold. It is completely blue with piercing black eyes on either side of its head. The legs of this magnificent creature are long and black, with what look like hairs of the finest thread, placed at even spaces down each side.

The thorax, the part next to its head, is large. It is not as slender as the abdomen, but it is very sleek, with patches of blue and black reflecting the brilliant sunlight.

As I watch, its head rotates and then suddenly it has disappeared hovering over the lake.

The other demoiselle fly still remains. This is not such a beautiful creature as the first, but it has striking markings. The wings are a dull brown in colour. They are much wider and not as long. They appear to be much more powerful than the lacy, delicate wings of the other fly. The abdomen of this creature is much thicker. It is dull brown, like the wings, but has flecks of mauve and grey. It appears, just as with the wings, to be much stronger, more substantial, and more useful.

The legs are very thick, although they still have the same appearance of delicacy about them, with the thin hairs vibrating rhythmically. The thorax is not as long as that of the other fly, but it is much thicker and more developed. It is green in colour with touches of brown, and gives the impression of strong armour plating.

The head is noble and bold. It is held high and the eyes are much larger and more powerful looking. It appears that this creature would be the male, as he appears stronger and more masculine in his appearance.

He waits motionless for a few seconds, then hovers over the lake, searching for the other fly, then disappears.

I am now left alone by the waters edge, the sun beating down, the flies once again busy in their search for food.

How schools have used this workshop

The following was the observation of a school's critical friend:

Primary school

There was considerable discussion of the introductory material, particularly the accounts of the demoiselle flies. Exemplar materials were then discussed in KS1 and KS2 groups, followed by some whole-staff discussion. The KS2 group had contrasting pieces of writing on 'The Trouble with Teacher'. One (girl's) piece was vastly superior to the other in terms of relevance, structure, vocabulary, handwriting, punctuation and spelling. However, the other (a boy's) had strengths in that he had at least one new idea on each line. It was not clear whether all staff judged the pieces according to the same criteria. However, some saw strengths and weaknesses in both pieces. This led to a discussion on the value, or otherwise, of setting and streaming to cope with such disparate performances.

The following was a school co-ordinator's comment in relation to the task materials:

Primary school

I was concerned that the English example in Task 1 would seem irrelevant to primary teachers, but it took little time and teachers recognised the issue.

Workshop 4: Self-assessment and peer-assessment

Aims

After completing this workshop, teachers should:

- understand the role of self-assessment and peer-assessment in improving pupils' learning;
- be able to create one or two of the self-assessment and peer-assessment strategies for use with pupils;
- be able to plan to implement these strategies.

Evidence from research

1   Learners must ultimately be responsible for their learning since no one else can do it for them. Thus assessment for learning must involve pupils. The awareness of learning and the ability of learners to direct it for themselves is of increasing importance in the context of encouraging lifelong learning (Assessment Reform Group, 1999).
2   Self-assessment has been defined as 'the process of reflecting on past experience, seeking to remember and understand what took place and attempting to gain a clear idea of what has been learned or achieved' (Munby et al., 1989).
3   In self-assessment pupils have to understand the criteria or standards that will be

used to assess their work, make judgements about their work in relation to these and any feedback from the teacher, and work out the implications of this for future action.

4   For self-assessment to work, it is important that pupils are given opportunities to reflect on the quality of their work against agreed standards. (These 'agreed' standards might be 'received' national curriculum standards or they might be negotiated in the classroom.) Pupils need to be supported to admit to difficulties without risk to their self-esteem. They need to be given time to work problems out and know that it is acceptable to consider a number of possible solutions before acting.

5   The move from assessment by teachers to self-assessment can be challenging and peer-assessment can help pupils to make this transition. Peer-assessment is valuable because it improves motivation, involves communication in pupils' natural language, encourages acceptance by pupils of criticism, strengthens pupil voice in feedback to the teacher, and frees teachers to stand back from activity and observe (Black *et al.*, 2003).

6   New learning strategies can be developed by scrutinising the work of others because it gives pupils a wider view of what is possible. Exploration of others' work allows pupils to see different ways of tackling the same task and, as a result, extending their own repertoire.

7   It is possible for pupils to become clearer about their own expectations through trying to explain strengths and weaknesses to others. This may result in the learning of new and better strategies.

8   Druckman and Swets (1988) argue that peer feedback is as, or more, influential than teacher feedback in obtaining lasting performance results, but *effective* learning will occur only if pupils are clear about what they know, understand and can do at the start of a piece of work and what they will know, understand and be able to do when they have completed the work (QCA, 2001).

9   Self-assessment and peer-assessment help pupils to become more effective learners by enabling them to reflect on: their knowledge of themselves as thinkers and learners; their understanding of the task in hand; ways in which they can improve their learning. In doing so, it contributes to increased self-esteem, motivation and personal responsibility for learning.

10 Successful self- and peer-assessment involves all three of the other key processes that are the focus of assessment for learning (see Workshops 1, 2 and 3):
   * developing classroom talk especially through questioning
   * feedback
   * sharing criteria of quality.

References

Assessment Reform Group (1999) *Assessment for Learning: beyond the black box.* Cambridge, University of Cambridge School of Education.

Black, P., Harrison, C., Lee, C., Marshall, B. and Wiliam, D. (2003) *Assessment for Learning: putting it into practice.* Maidenhead, Open University Press.

Druckman, D. and Swets, J. (1988). *Enhancing Human Performance.* Washington, DC, National Academy Press.

Munby, S. *et al.*, (1989) *Assessing and Recording Achievement.* Oxford, Blackwell.

QCA (2001) *Using Assessment to Raise Achievement in Mathematics: Key Stages 1, 2 and 3.* London, QCA.

Workshop tasks

This workshop consists of a pre-workshop task, three tasks and a follow-up task.

Pre-workshop task

In advance of the session, participants should be asked to think about self- and peer-assessment, e.g. what it might involve and how they currently, or might in the future, develop it in their subject or area of work.

Task 1: what do you currently do? (about 30 minutes)

Work with other colleagues in your key stage/department and identify ways in which you currently provide opportunities for peer- and self-assessment. How effective are these in relation to the claims made for the benefits of self- and peer-assessment?

Focus on one example and consider the extent to which this provides opportunities to:

1　help pupils understand the purposes of tasks;
2　help pupils understand the criteria by which they are to be assessed;
3　involve them in developing criteria for assessment;
4　involve them in reflecting against agreed criteria and identify ways in which they can improve;
5　provide opportunities for them to take some control of their learning;
6　help them to see learning as a continuous process by linking the present with past and future learning;
7　increase motivation and support the development of their self-concept.

Task 2: what does self-assessment look like in action? (about 20 minutes with 10 minutes whole-group discussion)

In groups of two to four, review the list of self-assessment strategies provided (see 'Task materials') and consider the extent to which one or two of them might be used by you. What would you need to do to ensure that:

(a)　they become embedded in your practice and
(b)　there is consistency in the pupils' experience in your key stage/department and the school?

Task 3: action (about 5 minutes)

In the light of your reflections during the workshop, write some individual notes about:

1　What self- and peer-assessment strategies will you try out in your own teaching? (It is important to select one or two examples and try these over a period of time.)
2　How will this be co-ordinated with other colleagues?
3　What will you need to do to prepare your pupils for effective peer- and self-evaluation?

Follow-up task: reflection on self- and peer-assessment in action

For this task, you will need to video self-assessment practice in the classroom – either in your classroom or a colleague's, with appropriate consent. Allow 5–10 minutes for video review, 10 minutes for paired discussion of the questions, and 5 minutes for a group review.

In pairs, review the video extract with the following questions in mind:

1   To what extent do the pupils use criteria?
2   To what extent do judgements focus on effort?
3   To what extent is the focus on surface features (e.g. layout, neatness)?
4   Are any suggestions made about ways in which the work might be improved?
5   What evidence is there that the pupils are able to take risks?

Task materials

Self-assessment and peer-assessment strategies

INVOLVING PUPILS IN MARKING

Pupils can mark their own work and that of others against clear criteria and learning intentions. The criteria can be developed as a class activity; this clarifies the teacher's expectations and involves the pupils in reflecting on how far their work fulfils these expectations. The aim of the activity should be to identify ways that the pupil whose work is being marked can move forward. (Good examples of this strategy are provided in the AAIA publication 'Pupils Learning from Teachers' responses' – see http://www.aaia.org.uk/_members/pdf/feedback.pdf.)

MARKING IN GROUPS

An alternative to marking individually is for pupils to do this as a group. The focus should be on a recently completed piece of work and members of the group should help one another to assess the work against agreed criteria and suggest ways in which the work could be improved.

MARKING AGAINST ANNOTATED EXAMPLES

Another useful marking strategy is for groups to work together to see how closely their work measures up against an 'ideal solution'. Whilst it will be important to emphasise that there could be many 'ideal solutions', group discussion should aim to help each pupil understand the extent to which their response achieves the criteria and what they can do to improve.

INDIVIDUAL SELF-ASSESSMENT SHEETS

These can be developed for some elements of a programme and invite pupils to reflect on the extent to which their work has achieved identified criteria. In the light of this they have to indicate what they need to do to improve.

TRAFFIC LIGHTS

This has proved a popular strategy and invites pupils to reflect on the current state of their learning in relation to a particular task or activity. If they feel confident that they understand a given piece of work, they use a green indicator (a marker, coloured pencil/crayon, card, or a sticker). If they are not quite sure of their understanding they use amber. If they are very uncertain, they use a red indicator. The idea here is that 'traffic lights' are used as an expression of a learner's confidence in their learning; it is not intended to be used as just another scoring system to assess their performance. This is a subtle but important distinction. In the light of their judgement, it is important that pupils then think about what they need to do to move from red/amber to green. Students indicating green could be used to advise those who used amber and the teacher can then work with those who used red. An alternative to the 'traffic lights' is to use three versions of smiley faces or post-it notes.

LAST FIVE MINUTES

At the start of a lesson, the teacher makes the purpose of the lesson clear and during the last five minutes one of the pupils explains what they have learned in the lesson. Others in the class question them about this.

QUESTIONS AND TASKS TO EXTEND UNDERSTANDING

At the end of a lesson or a unit of work, pupils can be invited to suggest questions that could be used to assess their understanding against the established criteria. These could become homework tasks, which could be assessed by pupils in ways described above.

GAUGING SELF-IMPROVEMENT AGAINST THEIR OWN PAST WORK

The same problem or task could be reintroduced from time to time, as part of a revision exercise, so that pupils can judge for themselves how much better or more sophisticated their reasoning is now than before. By returning to a problem or task and comparing current responses to those produced in the past they can develop an appreciation of their own mental growth and the development of new forms of thought and perspective.

PORTFOLIOS OF PAST WORK

Pupils could be invited to produce a class or subject portfolio of completed work that illustrates the standards expected. This could be regularly added to by drawing on examples from the above activities.

PRESENTATIONS

During the course of a unit of work, providing opportunities to present to the class allows individuals and groups to illustrate current understanding and progress. Self-assessment is involved in making decisions about what to include and how best to present. Feedback from teachers and peers contributes to the development of peer-assessment.

VIDEOING GROUP PRESENTATIONS

This allows pupils to reflect on and review their knowledge in the light of their own reflections and further feedback from other members of the class.

'PLAN, DO AND REVIEW'

This is a process developed in the High Scope Project for very young children. At the start of any activity the teacher works with the children to decide on the focus for a session. The children engage in the activity or task and then, at the end, time is allocated for them to work with the teacher to review what has been learned. Over time, this responsibility can be devolved to the children themselves.

IT'S OK NOT TO UNDERSTAND AND BE STUCK

An important element of developing the skills of self-assessment is how the teacher deals with situations where pupils find their work difficult. The language that teachers use is influential in building an acceptance that it is OK to find things difficult and that recognising this is an important aspect of learning. Consider ways in which you can get that message over to pupils. To supplement this teachers have found that introducing a framework for reflecting on learning can help develop confidence in pointing out areas which need support as well as those that have proved successful. For example, the following list of questions (perhaps using one or two at a time) can be used to start the process. It is usually best to relate these to the specific learning intentions of the lesson.

1 Have you learned anything new?
2 What were you most pleased with?
3 What did you find easy?
4 What did you find more difficult?
5 What helped you to solve your difficulty?
6 What can you do now that you couldn't do before?
7 What do you need more help with?
8 How would you change this activity for another group?
9 Do you have any questions?

How schools have used this workshop

Peer-assessment presents considerable challenges but the results are promising:

Secondary school

LSAs identified constraints and opportunities in relation to the use of peer-assessment in class:

(a) Lack of respect and trust among students, especially in Year 8. Fear of belittlement. Students wary of peer criticism.
(b) Students would engage in a restrained form of assessment: won't say anything horrible or critical to their friends.

However:

(c) Peer-assessment is a powerful tool. Students will need to be acculturated and this will need much preparation.
(d) Peer-assessment has the potential for turning around disaffected students as they perceive they have a greater stake in classroom lessons and learning.
(e) Need a change of culture: criticise the work, not the person.
(f) Need for sensitive feedback.

Secondary school

Peer-assessment:

- Departments that have tried this out have been pleased with the outcomes so far, and pupil response.
- At present, peer-assessment seems to be most effective with pupils at KS 4/5.
- It is clear that younger pupils need to be given time to develop skills. In this respect liaison with primaries could be crucial so that we build on what pupils are used to in this area.

Primary school

There was also a strong feeling that oral forms of peer- and self-assessment would be interesting to pursue (to avoid even more writing). The early years teachers felt that some of the suggested strategies might be difficult for their children but there was still scope for developing some of the ideas for their particular groups.

Workshop 5: How people learn

Aims

After completing this workshop, teachers should be able to:

1 review research evidence about how people learn;
2 use the notes describing three major clusters of learning theories to think about alternative ways to plan teaching;
3 critique these ideas;
4 plan an appropriate way of teaching a new unit for effective learning.

Evidence from research

1 Teaching is based on assumptions about how people learn although these assumptions are not always very explicit or based on sound evidence. Gradgrind, in Dickens's novel *Hard Times*, believed that children's minds were like little pitchers to be filled full of facts; the job of the teacher was to know a lot of facts and tell them to pupils whose job it was to memorise them. There are still a lot of people who hold this 'folk' perspective on learning.
2 Other common assumptions about learning have their origins in behaviourist psychology: (i) that a complex skill can be taught by breaking it up and teaching and testing the pieces separately; (ii) that an idea which is common in many contexts can be taught most economically by presenting it in abstract isolation so that it can then be applied in many situations; and (iii) that it is best to learn facts and basic skills first and not try for understanding, which will come later. A test composed of many short, 'atomised', out-of-context questions, and 'teaching to the test', are both consistent with this approach.

3 'Constructivist' theories look at the learning process quite differently. They focus attention on the mental models that a learner employs when responding to new information or to new problems. Learning always involves analysing and transforming any new information. Transformations of incoming ideas can only be achieved in the light of what the learner already knows and understands, so the reception of new knowledge depends on existing knowledge and understanding. This implies that teaching must start by exploring existing ideas and encouraging expression and defence of them; unless learners make their thinking explicit to others, and so to themselves, they cannot become aware of the need for conceptual modification. It follows that assessment for learning must be directed at the outset to reveal important aspects of understanding, and then provide contexts that challenge and develop pupils' ideas.

4 Those people who progress better in learning turn out to have better self-awareness and better strategies for self-regulation than their slower learning peers. Thus self-assessment becomes an important focus of assessment for learning. Students need to understand what it means to learn and they need to monitor how they go about planning, monitoring and revising, to reflect upon their learning and to learn to determine for themselves whether they understand. Such skills enhance meta-cognition, which is an essential strategic competence for learning.

5 The Russian psychologist, Vygotsky, emphasised that another important characteristic of learning is that it proceeds by interaction between the teacher (or more expert peer) and the learner, in a social context, mediated by language and promoted by the social norms that value the search for understanding. Wood *et al.* (1976) developed the implications of this for teaching by introducing the metaphor of 'scaffolding' – the teacher provides the scaffold for the building, but the building itself can only be constructed by the learner. In this supportive role, the teacher has to discern the potential of the learner to advance in understanding, so that new challenges are neither too trivial nor too demanding.

6 Since a learner's response will be sensitive to the language and social context of any communication, teaching and assessments have to be carefully framed, both in their language and context of presentation, if they are to avoid bias, i.e. unfair effects on those from particular gender, social, ethnic or linguistic groups.

7 Recent developments in learning theory have come from socio-cultural theorists, including anthropologists, who have observed that people learn through participating in 'communities of practice', like apprentices. Through membership and activity they come to understand what to pay attention to and what counts as quality in a particular group – it is 'situated'. This is an important consideration for teachers in schools because what is required in one subject, for example writing descriptive prose in English, may not be the same as, say, writing up an experiment in science.

8 The idea of 'distributed cognition' emphasises that the knowledge of the group is rarely, if ever, held in the head of a single individual. All the individuals know rather different things, but when their collective expertise is put to work they can be productive in a way that is greater than the sum of the individuals. The notion that learning involves collaborative problem-solving is an important one for teachers in schools and suggests that group work is not an optional extra but essential for learning.

9 The idea of learning as activity involving a division of labour among people with different roles is associated with a version of the socio-cultural perspective called activity theory. This emphasises the importance of the use of tools by learners and teachers. These can be artefacts such as books and equipment but they can also be social, cultural or conceptual tools such as key ideas or processes. A focus for

assessment of learning is therefore the extent to which learners choose and use tools effectively.

10 In this very brief account of learning theory, you may have detected three main strands or perspectives on learning theory. They have acquired a variety of labels but the three most often used are:
- behaviourist learning theory
- cognitive constructivist learning theory
- socio-cultural learning theory.

Watkins (2003), in a very accessible little guide for teachers, refers to these as:
- Learning is Being Taught (LBT).
- Learning is Individual Sense-making (LIS).
- Learning is Building Knowledge as part of doing things with Others (LBKO).

11 Anna Sfard (1998) pointed out that underpinning all this theoretical discussion are two key metaphors: a metaphor of acquisition and a metaphor of participation. She also pointed out how dangerous it can be to 'show too great a devotion to one particular metaphor'. The same might be said of learning theory more generally. Teachers will probably find a practical use at some time for all three theories: behaviourist, constructivist, and socio-cultural.

References

Bransford, J.A., Brown, A. and Cocking, R. (1999) *How People Learn: brain, mind, experience and school.* Washington, DC, National Academy Press.

Bredo, E. (1993) The Social Construction of Learning. In G. D. Phye (ed.) *Handbook of Academic Learning: construction of knowledge.* San Diego, CA, Academic Press.

James, M. (2006) Assessment, Teaching and Theories of Learning. In J. Gardner (ed.) *Assessment and Learning.* London, Sage Publications.

Sfard, A. (1998) On Two Metaphors for Learning and the Dangers of Choosing Just One. *Educational Researcher*, May, pp. 4–13.

Watkins, C. (2003) *Learning: a sense-maker's guide.* London, Association of Teachers and Lecturers.

Wood, D (1998). *How Children Think and Learn: the social contexts of cognitive development* (2nd Edition). Oxford, Blackwell.

Wood, D., Bruner, J., S, and Ross, G. (1976) The Role of Tutoring in Problem Solving. *Journal of Child Psychology and Psychiatry*, 17, pp. 89–100.

Note: Most of these are overviews rather than about specific theories. If you have time to read only one or two of these references, read Watkins (2003) first, because this is an easy way in, followed by Bransford *et al.* (1999).

Workshop tasks

This workshop consists of a pre-workshop task, an introduction, two tasks and a follow-up task.

Pre-workshop task

Each participant should collect and bring to the workshop four copies of a topic, unit or theme that they will be teaching in the next half-term.

INTRODUCTION (ABOUT 10 MINUTES)

Teachers need to think about how children learn in order to plan their teaching. This is *not* a question of learning styles but relates to more fundamental ideas about the ways that *all* people learn. Look at the notes on theories of learning (see 'Task materials', pages 54–55) and relate these to the 'Evidence from research' (pages 50–52). The notes on learning theories were derived partly from the chapter by Eric Bredo (1993), given in the references. They summarise each of the three clusters of theories in terms of some key characteristics:

- key ideas about learning
- implications for teaching
- implications for differentiation
- the nature of achievement
- implications for assessment
- key theorists
- associated philosophical movements.

Task 1: theory in practice: a thought experiment (about 45 minutes)

1 Staff should divide into three groups (or multiples of three) to form one or more 'behaviourist' groups, 'cognitive constructivist' groups, and 'socio-cultural' groups. Each group needs a copy of the relevant notes.
2 As a whole group, choose a recent government directive or curriculum initiative (e.g. some time ago the Secretary of State suggested the need for a citizenship programme for new immigrants or asylum seekers).
3 Look at the summary, in the notes, of the cluster of learning theories that your group has been given.
4 Now, from the perspective of the theory on your chart, consider the advice that you would offer on a programme for teaching the initiative. Write an outline on a flip-chart sheet.
5 Present and defend your ideas to the other groups, and critique theirs from the perspective of 'your' theory.
6 This is a difficult activity and the worked example (see 'Task materials') may help.

Task 2: planning practice using theory (about 30 minutes)

1 In pairs, and using the pre-workshop task, discuss the best ways to teach the unit/topic to be taught in the next term, drawing on ideas from learning theory.
2 Make an action plan.

Follow-up task: implementing and reviewing action

1 Implement over the next half-term or so. This needs to be planned over a realistic timescale with targets and scheduled review dates.
2 Review and amend in consultation with your partner.

Task materials

Notes on theories of learning

BEHAVIOURIST THEORIES

Key ideas about learning   Environment is the determining factor. Learning is conditioned response to external stimuli. Complex wholes are assembled out of parts. This theory has no concept of mind, intelligence, ego etc. – it is only interested in observable behaviour.

Implications for teaching   The teacher's role is to train people to respond to instruction correctly and rapidly. Basic skills are introduced before complex skills. Positive feedback and correction of mistakes are used to make the connections between stimulus and response.

Implications for differentiation   Students can be taught in homogenous groups according to level of skill, or individually according to rate of progress through a differentiated programme, based on a fixed hierarchy of skill acquisition.

Nature of achievement   The accumulation of skills and facts, in a given subject, is demonstrated in speedy performance and the formation of habits.

Implications for assessment   Progress is measured through timed tests with items taken from different levels in a skill hierarchy (constructed by decomposition).

Key theorists   Watson; Skinner; Pavlov; Thorndike.

Associated philosophical movements   positivism; empiricism; technicism; managerialism.

COGNITIVE CONSTRUCTIVIST THEORIES

Key ideas about learning   Learning is determined by what goes on in people's heads. The focus is on how people construct meaning and make sense of the world through organising concepts and principles in schemata (mental models). There is an emphasis on conceptual knowledge. Problem-solving is seen as the context for knowledge construction, although strategies for problem-solving and reasoning are important.

Implications for teaching   The role of the teacher is to help 'novices' to acquire 'expert' understanding and solve given problems by symbolic manipulation with 'less search'.

Implications for differentiation   People's constructions of knowledge vary with past experience, so teachers need to take account of individual and group differences in present understanding in order to 'scaffold' future learning.

Nature of achievement   Understanding and competence in relation to:

- skills, facts, concepts and principles
- strategies and procedures
- meta-cognition, self-monitoring and self-regulation.

Implications for assessment   It is necessary to elicit students' mental models (through open-ended assignments, thinking-aloud protocols, concept-mapping) and give opportunities to apply concepts and strategies in novel situations.

Key theorists   Piaget; Chomsky; Bruner (but his later work engages with the socio-cultural perspective); Hirst; H. Simon.

Associated philosophical movements   positivism; rationalism; humanism.

SOCIO-CULTURAL THEORIES

Key ideas about learning   Learning occurs in interaction between the individual and the environment. Thinking is conducted through actions that alter the situation and the situation changes the thinking. Learning involves participation and problem-solving and is not necessarily the property of an individual but shared within the social group (distributed cognition). The collective knowledge of the group/organisation is greater than the sum of the knowledge of individuals.

Implications for teaching   The teacher needs to create an environment in which people can be stimulated to think and act in authentic tasks (like apprentices) beyond their current level of competence. It is important to find activities that a person can complete with assistance but not alone. The teacher 'scaffolds' the learning for the pupil. Tasks need to be collaborative and pupils need to be involved in the generation of problems and solutions. Teachers and pupils jointly solve problems and all develop their skill and understanding.

Implications for differentiation   Differentiation is intrinsic to learning because problems and actions are generated as social situations change. Since neither the environment nor the internal organisation of the individual is fixed, differentiation as a contrived strategy is not relevant. Individuals can have different levels of participation in activity and all move to increased participation.

Nature of achievement   Achievement is defined as engaged participation in ways that others find appropriate, i.e. seeing the world in a particular way and acting accordingly – shaping and being shaped by a community of practice. Knowledge needs to be seen in relation to context, and understanding cannot be judged in absolute terms; it will change as circumstances change.

Implications for assessment   Learning needs to be inferred from active participation in authentic (real-world) projects. Focus is on how well people use the resources or tools (intellectual, human, material) available to them to formulate problems, work productively and evaluate their efforts.

Key theorists   W. James; Dewey; Mead; Dreyfus; Vygotsky; Rogoff; Lave; E. Wenger; Engeström

Associated philosophical movements   pragmatism; functionalism; social democratic/progressivist politics; existentialism; phenomenology; Marxist dialecticism; modernism; communitarianism.

Worked examples

Source: James, M. (2006) Assessment, Teaching and Theories of Learning. In J. Gardner (ed.) *Assessment and Learning*. London, Sage Publications. Reprinted here with permission.

Consider the following examples. They are written as caricatures of particular approaches in order to provide a basis for subsequent discussion. In reality, the differences are unlikely to be so stark and teachers often blend approaches. The focus of the examples is a secondary school teacher who has just received a new student into her English class. He has recently arrived in the country and English is an additional language for him although he speaks English reasonably well. The teacher wants to assess his writing. If she chooses one of the following approaches what would it say about her model of knowledge, learning and assessment?

Example 1

She sits him in a quiet room by himself and sets him a timed test that consists of short-answer questions asking him, without recourse to reference material or access to other students, to: identify parts of given sentences (nouns, verbs, articles, connectives); make a list of adjectives to describe nouns; punctuate sentences; spell a list of ten words in a hierarchy of difficulty; write three sentences describing a favourite animal or place; write the opening paragraph of a story. She then marks these using a marking scheme (scoring rubric), which enables her to identify incorrect answers or weaknesses and compare his performance with others in the class. As a result she places him in a group with others at a similar level and then provides this group with additional exercises to practise performance in areas of weakness. When he shows improvement she is liberal with her praise and then moves on to the next set of skills to be learnt. Learning by rote and practice are a dominant feature of this approach.

Example 2

As part of her class teaching, she has been covering work on 'genre' in the programme of study. Her current focus is narrative and especially the aspect of temporal sequencing. The class has been reading J.R.R. Tolkien's *The Hobbit* and she used this as a stimulus for their own writing of stories of journeys in search of treasure. The students discuss the qualities of *The Hobbit* that make it a good story, including structure, plot, characterisation, use of language and dramatic tension (all key concepts to be understood). These they note as things to consider in their own writing. Using a writing frame they first plan their stories and then try out opening paragraphs. They write their stories over a series of lessons. At draft stages they review their work, individually, with the teacher, and through peer discussion, using the criteria they have developed. Then they redraft to improve their work using the feedback they have received. The teacher monitors this activity throughout and observes that her new student has a rich experience of travel to draw on, although some of those experiences have been negative and need to be handled sensitively. With English as an additional language he knows more than he can say and needs to be helped to acquire a wider vocabulary. He also has problems with sequencing which she thinks could indicate a specific learning difficulty or a different cultural conception of time. She makes a mental note to observe this in future activities. In the meantime she decides to provide lots of opportunities for him to engage in classroom talk to help with the first difficulty. To help with the sequencing difficulty, she suggests that he writes topic sentences on card and cuts them out so that he can physically move them round his table until he gets them in a satisfactory order. When his story is complete, the student is asked to record his own self-evaluation and the teacher makes comments on this and his work which they discuss together to decide next steps. She does not make much use of praise or numerical scores or grades because, by making learning explicit, he understands the nature and substance of the progress he has made.

Example 3

The teacher regards one of her main aims as helping to develop her students as writers. To this end she constructs her classroom as a writing workshop. The new student is invited to join this workshop and all participants, including the teacher and any learning support assistants, are involved, on this occasion, in writing stories for children of a different age to themselves. Although their own writing, or the writing of others, including established authors, is used to stimulate thinking and writing, all members in the group, from the most expert to the most novice, are encouraged to set their own goals and to choose an individual or group task that will be challenging but achievable with the help of the knowledge and skill of others in the group. There is no concept of a single, specific goal to be achieved or a performance 'gap' to be closed but rather a 'horizon of possibilities' to be reached. The broad learning goal is for all members of the group to develop their *identities* as writers. By participating together in the activity of writing, each member of the group has the opportunity to learn from the way others tackle the tasks (rather than being told how to do things). Different members of the group take on the role of student and teacher according to the particular challenges of a given activity. For example, if the teacher wants to write a story for young people, she might need to learn about street language from her students; thus they become her teachers. At intervals the members of the group read their work to the rest and the group appraise it, drawing on the criteria they use to judge what counts as good work. These criteria may be those shared by writers more generally (as in examples 1 and 2 above) but the dynamic of the group might allow new criteria to emerge and be accepted as norms for this group. For example, the introduction of a new student member with a different cultural background could encourage more experimental work in the group as a whole. The model is in some respects similar to apprenticeship models, although these tend to be associated with the preservation and maintenance of guild knowledge. In other respects it goes beyond this and, like the University of East Anglia's well-known creative writing course, it seeks to foster creativity. Our new student begins by being a peripheral participant in this writing workshop, observing and learning from what others do, but gradually he is brought into the group and becomes a full participating member. Assessment in this context is ongoing, continuous, shared by all participants (not just the preserve of the teacher) but linked very specifically to the particular activity. There is often less concern to make general statements about competence and more concern to appraise the quality of the particular performance or artefact, and the process of producing it. It is considered especially important to evaluate how well the student has used the resources (tools) available to him, in terms of materials, technology, people, language and ideas, to solve the particular problems he faced. The learning is focused on an authentic project so one of the most important indicators of success will be whether the audience for the stories produced (other children) respond to them positively. Their response will also provide key formative feedback to be used by the individual student and the group in future projects. The role of the English teacher is therefore not as final arbiter of quality but as 'more expert other' and 'guide on the side'. Learning outcomes are best recorded and demonstrated to others through portfolios of work, rather like those produced by art students, or through the vehicle of the 'masterpiece' (the 'piece for the master craftsman' designed to be a demonstration of the best of which the apprentice is capable – also a model for the doctoral thesis).

Part III   Learning across and beyond the school

Overview

This section is a toolbox containing a number of instruments that you can use to explore issues at the interface of classroom and whole-school practice. Promoting learning how to learn by pupils in classrooms represents a considerable innovation in teachers' practices. This requires teachers to learn these new practices; such learning needs to be encouraged by a supportive school culture. School leaders need, therefore, to consider how they can support teachers' professional learning and how they can develop a school environment and ethos conducive to the development of learning how to learn by pupils and teachers in classrooms. One way forward is to begin by finding out how staff engage in professional learning and how supportive they perceive school management systems and practices to be. On this basis you can work out what may need to be done to make improvements.

These features of the school, and the links between them, can be investigated by using the questionnaires included in this book. Questionnaire A, in Part I (pages 20–24), can help you investigate the classroom assessment practices that teachers value and practise in your school. Questionnaire B, in this Part (pages 68–72), can help you to find out about the professional learning practices which staff engage in and value. Questionnaire C, also in this Part (pages 73–76), can be used to inquire into staff perceptions of school culture and ethos. If you ask teachers to complete all three questionnaires, you can analyse the relationships in their responses between these three aspects. On the website, at http://www.learntolearn.ac.uk, you will find electronic versions of these questionnaires and also separate versions of question-naires for primary and secondary schools which combine the three questionnaires. (Look for 'Self-evaluation resources'.) These versions may be helpful if you want to examine links, although this combined questionnaire takes about 45 minutes for teachers to complete. The separate versions in this book take about 15 minutes each.

As in Part I, in relation to the questionnaire about classroom assessment practices (pages 20–24), we include here some tables of results from teachers who completed the questionnaires on professional learning and school management and culture. The results are from around 1,000 teachers and school managers in 32 primary and secondary schools. As before, the tables cluster the items together in factors and show percentage responses to the two most positive categories in our 'values' and 'practice' scales. On the practice scale, staff were asked to report their perception of practice across the school. These tables enable you to see value–practice gaps. You should bear in mind that school differences are ironed out because these tables aggregate scores from teachers across a number of schools. However, they may be useful to you in comparing your results with a wider sample.

Dimensions of teachers' learning

Factor B1: Inquiry

Using and responding to different sources of evidence; carrying out joint research and evaluation with colleagues

Item		Values (%) Important/ crucial	Practices (%) Some/ most staff
2	Staff draw on good practice from other schools as a means to further their own professional development.	95	70
3	Staff read research reports as one source of useful ideas for improving their practice.	71	42
4	Staff use the web as one source of useful ideas for improving their practice.	79	80
5	Pupils are consulted about how they learn most effectively.	89	51
6	Staff relate what works in their own practice to research findings.	62	33
12	Staff modify their practice in the light of published research evidence.	60	34
15	Staff carry out joint research/evaluation with one or more colleagues as a way of improving practice.	81	48

Factor B2: Building social capital

Learning, working, supporting and talking with each other

Item		Values (%) Important/ crucial	Practices (%) Some/ most staff
16	Staff regularly collaborate to plan their teaching.	92	78
19	If staff have a problem with their teaching they usually turn to colleagues for help.	99	90
20	Teachers suggest ideas or approaches for colleagues to try out in class.	98	92
21	Teachers make collective agreements to test out new ideas.	88	72
22	Teachers discuss openly with colleagues what and how they are learning.	85	70
23	Staff frequently use informal opportunities to discuss how pupils learn.	90	80
24	Staff offer one another reassurance and support.	99	95

Factor B3: Critical and responsive learning

Through reflection, self-evaluation, experimentation and by responding to feedback

Item		Values (%) Important/ crucial	Practices (%) Some/ most staff
7	Staff are able to see how practices that work in one context might be adapted to other contexts.	93	77
9	Staff reflect on their practice as a way of identifying professional learning needs.	95	86
10	Staff experiment with their practice as a conscious strategy for improving classroom teaching and learning.	98	84
11	Staff modify their practice in the light of feedback from their pupils.	90	65
13	Staff modify their practice in the light of evidence from self-evaluations of their classroom practice.	97	78
14	Staff modify their practice in the light of evidence from evaluations of their classroom practice by managers or other colleagues.	94	85

Factor B4: Valuing learning

Item		Values (%) Important/ crucial	Practices (%) Some/ most staff
1	Staff as well as pupils learn in this school.	99	95
25	Staff believe that all pupils are capable of learning.	99	95
26	Pupils in this school enjoy learning.	99	91
27	Pupil success is regularly celebrated.	99	96

Dimensions of school management systems

Factor C1: Deciding and acting together

Involving staff in decision-making and using their professional know-how in the formulation and critical evaluation of school policy

Item		Values (%) Important/ crucial	Practices (%) Often/ mostly true
5	There are processes for involving all staff in decision-making.	95	58
6	Teachers' professional know-how is used in the formulation of school policy and goals.	97	71
7	Teachers' professional know-how is used in the formulation of school policy, even where this leads to a questioning of established rules, procedures and practices.	94	56
8	Opportunities are provided for teachers to critically evaluate school policy.	94	49
9	Staff are actively involved in evaluating school policy.	93	53
10	Staff participate in important decision-making.	94	50

Factor C2: Developing a sense of where we are going

Clear communication by senior management of a clear vision and the fostering of staff commitment to the whole school based on good working knowledge among staff of school development priorities which they view as relevant and useful for learning and teaching

Item		Values (%) Important/ crucial	Practices (%) Often/ mostly true
1	Senior management communicates a clear vision of where the school is going.	97	82
2	Staff have a commitment to the whole school as well as to their department, key stage and/or year group.	99	88
3	Senior management promotes commitment among staff to the whole school as well as to the department, key stage and/or year group.	98	79
12	Staff have a good working knowledge of the School Development Plan.	90	67
13	Staff see the School Development Plan as relevant and useful to learning and teaching.	84	57
14	Staff development time is used effectively to realise School Development Plan priorities.	90	62

Factor C3: Supporting professional development

Providing formal and informal training opportunities so that teachers, for example, can develop skills to assess their pupils work in ways that move them on in their learning, and to observe learning as it happens in the classroom.

Item		Values (%) Important/ crucial	Practices (%) Often/ mostly true
16	The school provides cover to allow staff joint planning time.	90	33
17	Teachers are encouraged to experiment with new ideas as a way of promoting professional growth.	97	75
18	Formal training provides opportunities for teachers to develop professionally.	97	82
19	Teachers are helped to develop skills to assess pupils' work in ways that move their pupils on in their learning.	99	68
20	Teachers are helped to develop skills to observe learning as it happens in the classroom.	97	48
26	Learning how to learn is an issue discussed in staff development time.	93	54

Factor C4: Auditing expertise and supporting networking

Information is collected on practices that staff themselves think they do effectively, and on informal teacher networking in which they play an active role. Teachers are supported in sharing practice with other schools through networking.

Item		Values (%) Important/ crucial	Practices (%) Often/ mostly true
21	Management supports teachers in sharing practice with other schools through networking.	85	45
22	Information is collected from teachers on those aspects of their work that they themselves think they do effectively.	86	38
23	Information is collected from teachers on effective ways they promote learning to learn skills and knowledge among their pupils.	90	37
24	Information is collected from teachers on informal teacher networking in which they play an active role.	69	29
25	Teacher-initiated networking is an integral element of staff development.	76	40

For the teachers who completed our surveys we looked at associations between factors on the different dimensions. This had interesting results (see Figure 1).

On the right of this figure are the three classroom assessment factors, described in Part I of this book. In the middle is the teacher learning factor – inquiry – that we found to be key to implementing AfL in the classroom, particularly 'promoting learning autonomy' in pupils. Teachers said this was important but the most difficult to achieve. On the left are the most crucial school management factors for encouraging

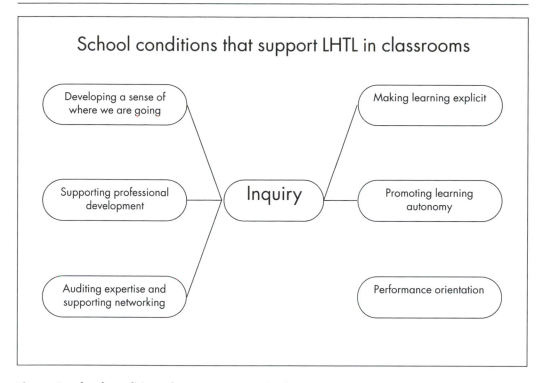

Figure 1: school conditions that support LHTL in classrooms

teachers' learning through classroom focused inquiry. This represents a linked chain of association.

Therefore, what appear to be important, at the level of the school, for developing AfL and LHTL practice in classrooms are: (a) a clear sense of direction – there is communication within the school of a clear vision, there is also commitment among staff to that vision; (b) systems of support for professional development – teachers released to plan together, they are encouraged to experiment and to take risks with their practice along with a range of other learning opportunities; and (c) the management of knowledge – expertise is audited, schools have systems for locating the strengths of staff as a basis for managing staff expertise and building on it through support for internal and external networking.

Above all, the key school condition for the classroom promotion of learning how to learn appears to be the development and support for teachers to carry out classroom-based inquiry into what they and their pupils are doing and learning.

This then provides a strong rationale for providing a 'box' of tools for learning at school level to support learning in classrooms. The premise is that if schools are to be learning communities they need to inquire critically into practice, test 'the way we do things round here' against evidence, and share thinking in a climate which is welcoming of challenge and diversity. If, for pupils, learning *how* to learn means standing back from your own learning to understand its deeper processes and principles, then the LHTL school is one in which staff not only learn together but are interested and enabled to take a wider perspective on how a school can share and profit from its own learning.

In the toolbox that we offer below, the staff questionnaires (B and C) are central. These are intended to be completed by all staff – teachers, teaching assistants and school leaders. The purpose of these surveys is to probe the nature of the school culture through a series of statements about learning at pupil, teacher and whole-school level. These ask for judgements about current practice in relation to their importance for the school. They also require people to respond with their own view but at times to assess their colleagues' practices and attitudes. While responses to each statement may of themselves be revealing, we are able to get a more developed picture as we examine how single items cluster together to give us 'factors'.

The data which questionnaire responses yield are, of course, open to a variety of interpretations and are of limited value without further elaboration and interpretative dialogue. In other words the questionnaire data are a starting point rather than an end point of inquiry, potentially formative rather than summative, diagnostic but only to the degree to which they are subjected to further, more fine-grained, inquiry.

The other tools in this toolbox are designed to support that further inquiry. They assume a context in which dialogue can occur whether within a leadership team, a small staff group, an INSET session or a whole-staff workshop, for example. They may be managed, or facilitated, by a member of staff, or by a critical friend external to the school. They may be used in conjunction (one or more tools in sequence) and invite adaptation to the school's own particular circumstances, needs and priorities.

Reflecting on the survey data

Two tools are provided to help staff engage with the factors that underpin the survey instrument. The first of these tools is a prompt designed to scan the survey results, focusing on places where there are gaps between expectation and current practice, and then focusing on one or more areas for more detailed discussion and strategic planning. The second of these also focuses on factors with a similar aim of helping people to gain more familiarity with the factors through a raised awareness of diverging views and sources of evidence. This second exercise is useful for a body such as governors, in introducing them to key concepts through an inclusive, engaging and challenging activity. It is useful to build into both activities a time at the end to stand back and review the process of discussion and any decision-making that flowed from the activity. It is here that a facilitator or external critical friend may play a key role.

Exploring school cultures

Many of the tools focus on school culture. In all of the following, the survey instrument, its factors, and its individual items may be an important point of cross reference as the dialogue proceeds.

The matrix suggests four types of culture. Its premise is that individual teachers may either privatise, or share, their thinking and practice (a broadening dimension) and/or may strengthen and enhance their practice (a deepening dimension). This may be done individually or collectively, the collective dimension (deep and broad) being the goal of the LHTL school. This may provoke discussion on aspects of school life which tend to broaden or deepen.

Through the eyes of the NQT, while lending itself to an activity, may serve as a set of guidelines or prompts for a school's staff to see themselves through a different lens. It may sit in the background as a reference point to return to in the course of discussion or along with other tools. It may, of course, also be used as a group activity, to stimulate discussion about how a school can move more systemically towards becoming an LHTL school.

Critical incident analysis focuses on specific incidents which may reflect aspects of a school's culture which impact on learning. Creating dialogue about these instances can help teachers, pupils, and perhaps parents and governors, to reflect on the causes, effects and implications of doing things in certain ways – and considering the alternatives.

A culture of shared leadership

Two activities focus on a culture of shared leadership. One uses Sergiovanni's (2001) terminology of *Leadership density* to examine the extent to which 'stakeholders' (teachers, pupils, parents and other groups) feel they can play a part in influencing process and outcomes at whole-school level. It helps in conceptual ground clearing on issues of expectations, authority and forms of knowledge. Thinking through these issues with the help of a matrix tool, potential for sharing of knowledge, authority and influence may be identified. This may be a natural lead in to the second activity which is concerned with *Leadership tasks.* Using the medium of a card 'game', groups of staff explore what constitutes sharing of leadership and search for agreement on strategic approaches to a more collaborative culture. Again, the survey questions and factors may be returned to as source of evidence or cross reference.

Exploring teaching

One activity included provides teachers with strategies for evaluating teaching and forms the basis for a dialogue about teaching and learning. *Peer observation* is a tried-and-tested strategy which, if managed appropriately, can be a source of professional learning rather than simply a strategy for monitoring.

Another version of peer observation is known as 'research lesson study' which originated in Japan. This approach has been developed by Pete Dudley alongside the Learning How to Learn Project (see http://www.tlrp.org/proj/phase111/rtfdudley.htm). Guidance booklets and a DVD that he developed, called 'Getting Started with Research Lessons', are available from NCSL and CfBT.

Recasting outcomes: the penultimate activity in this toolbox raises the issue of outcomes. In a climate where outcomes are widely taken as equivalent to attainment data, a recasting of the concept may help to widen perspectives, to consider how differently pupil, teacher and organisational outcomes might be conceived and what LHTL as a whole-school outcome might mean.

Finally, we include a version of the *Network-mapping tool* that we developed to help us understand how educational networks are configured and operate. This can be used to understand the wider network within which a school is operating. Despite all that is claimed for the power of networking, we discovered that what constitutes a network is poorly understood – particularly with respect to educational organisations. A network can be thought of as made up of those people, groups, organisations and communities (i.e. nodes) with whom people in the organisation connect. The connections (i.e. links) should include all methods of communication and networking activities with which the organisation is involved. This mapping tool was developed in the LHTL project to help expose such educational networks, using the perspectives of one or more school leaders. It is a flexible tool that provides a snapshot and can be used either to elicit an individual's roles and activity or their perceptions of their organisation's roles and activity. (The latter approach was the one used by the project.) It allows individuals to represent visually complex interactions on one A3 sheet of paper.

In the project, network maps were generated as the focus of a semi-structured interview which was tape recorded. The transcripts and maps were analysed descriptively using a standard form by a researcher; feedback of this analysis was presented to the map compilers for comment and verification. The maps were revisited one year after their compilation and change discussed. The task is most meaningful when set by someone who, in the first stages, will be acting as a facilitator but who, later, can take a more active, probing role. The process of constructing the network map has itself value to the map compiler but more value still will be gained if time is given to analyse and then revisit the map in conversation with someone else.

Adapting tools

The tools provided here may be used in the form they are given or they may be developed, adding or subtracting items, changing content or structure. Tools may also be adapted from one context to another. For example, the critical incident analysis, illustrated here at classroom level, is a well-tried instrument at whole-school level to help identify what went wrong, the locus of responsibility, what options existed but were not used, and what may be learned from the experience. The card game exploring shared leadership suggests endless possibilities for adaptation to different topics and uses.

Reference

Sergiovanni, T. (2001) *Leadership: What's in it for Schools?* London, RoutledgeFalmer.

Materials

We begin this collection of school-level tools by reproducing the *Staff questionnaire B: Professional learning practices and values*, and *Staff questionnaire C: School management practices and values*. These questionnaires can be photocopied from the materials given here or they can be downloaded from the website. Schools are encouraged to do their own analyses of the responses in ways that suit their purposes. However, as with Questionnaire A, in Part I, spreadsheets can be downloaded from the project website to help with analysis of school data. Instructions about how to produce data reports, which will compare a school's results with those for our project sample, are also available.

For schools that choose to do their own analysis, the factor tables, given above, provide a basis for comparison, albeit with the cautions we expressed in Part I. Values–practice gaps and patterns of similarity or difference across groups of staff might be helpful in deciding where to put effort in developing practice in school. The activities in this school-level toolbox are 'tagged' to our factors in order to assist choice of the activities that may be of most help in tackling the issues identified through the use of the questionnaires, or by other means.

The set of tools follows the questionnaires.

Tool 1: Staff questionnaire B: Professional learning practices and values

Completing the questionnaire

1. Staff questionnaire B consists of 28 statements. Each statement relates to an aspect of teachers' practices and beliefs about professional learning.

2. There are two scales for each of the 28 statements: scale X and scale Y. You are asked to tick one box only under scale X and one box only under scale Y for each statement.

3. Please note that scale X, on the left hand side, is *not about you*. Scale X is *about your colleagues'* practices as you perceive them.

4. If you are unable to make a judgement about colleagues' practices in relation to a statement, please tick the 'Don't know' box in scale X.

5. Scale Y, on the right hand side, asks you to tell us about your values: how important you regard each of the listed beliefs and practices for creating opportunities for pupils to learn. Or, do you think the particular practice is bad practice? In this case you would tick the box in the fifth column in scale Y.

6. Please just tick one box in scale X and one box in scale Y.

Example

SCALE X This school now					Professional learning practices and beliefs of colleagues	SCALE Y How important are these practices and beliefs for creating opportunities for pupils to learn?			
(This is about your colleagues!)						(This is about your values)			
True of no staff	True of few staff	True of some staff	True of most staff	Don't know		Not at all important	Of limited importance	Important	Crucial	Bad practice!
☐	☐	☐	✔	☐	Staff participate actively in teacher networks with colleagues.	☐	☐	☐	✔	☐

This respondent thinks that most staff in his school actively participate in informal teacher networks with colleagues. (S)he also thinks that networking among colleagues is crucial for creating opportunities for pupils to learn.
Please complete the questionnaire now.

SCALE X
This school now

(About your colleagues!)

SCALE Y
How important are these practices and beliefs for creating opportunities for pupils to learn?

(About your values)

Scale Y: Not at all important	Of limited importance	Important	Crucial	Bad practice!	Professional learning practices and beliefs of colleagues	Scale X: True of no staff	True of few staff	True of some staff	True of most staff	Don't know
☐	☐	☐	☐	☐	1. Staff as well as pupils learn in this school.	☐	☐	☐	☐	☐
☐	☐	☐	☐	☐	2. Staff draw on good practice from other schools as a means to further their own professional development.	☐	☐	☐	☐	☐
☐	☐	☐	☐	☐	3. Staff read research reports as one source of useful ideas for improving their practice.	☐	☐	☐	☐	☐
☐	☐	☐	☐	☐	4. Staff use the web as one source of useful ideas for improving their practice.	☐	☐	☐	☐	☐
☐	☐	☐	☐	☐	5. Pupils are consulted about how they learn most effectively.	☐	☐	☐	☐	☐
☐	☐	☐	☐	☐	6. Staff relate what works in their own practice to research findings.	☐	☐	☐	☐	☐
☐	☐	☐	☐	☐	7. Staff are able to see how practices that work in one context might be adapted to other contexts.	☐	☐	☐	☐	☐
☐	☐	☐	☐	☐	8. Staff use insights from their professional learning to feed into school policy development.	☐	☐	☐	☐	☐

SCALE X
This school now
Professional learning practices and beliefs of colleagues

(About your colleagues!)

SCALE Y
How important are these practices and beliefs for creating opportunities for pupils to learn?

(About your values)

Professional learning practices and beliefs of colleagues	True of no staff	True of few staff	True of some staff	True of most staff	Don't know	Not at all important	Of limited importance	Important	Crucial	Bad practice!
9. Staff reflect on their practice as a way of identifying professional learning needs.	☐	☐	☐	☐	☐	☐	☐	☐	☐	☐
10. Staff experiment with their practice as a conscious strategy for improving classroom teaching and learning.	☐	☐	☐	☐	☐	☐	☐	☐	☐	☐
11. Staff modify their practice in the light of feedback from their pupils.	☐	☐	☐	☐	☐	☐	☐	☐	☐	☐
12. Staff modify their practice in the light of published research evidence.	☐	☐	☐	☐	☐	☐	☐	☐	☐	☐
13. Staff modify their practice in the light of evidence from self-evaluations of their classroom practice.	☐	☐	☐	☐	☐	☐	☐	☐	☐	☐
14. Staff modify their practice in the light of evidence from evaluations of their classroom practice by managers or other colleagues.	☐	☐	☐	☐	☐	☐	☐	☐	☐	☐

SCALE Y
How important are these practices and beliefs for creating opportunities for pupils to learn?

(About your values)

Professional learning practices and beliefs of colleagues

SCALE X
This school now

(About your colleagues!)

	Not at all important	Of limited importance	Important	Crucial	Bad practice!	Statement	Don't know	True of most staff	True of some staff	True of few staff	True of no staff
	☐	☐	☐	☐	☐	15. Staff carry out joint research/evaluation with one or more colleagues as a way of improving their practice.	☐	☐	☐	☐	☐
	☐	☐	☐	☐	☐	16. Staff regularly collaborate to plan their teaching.	☐	☐	☐	☐	☐
	☐	☐	☐	☐	☐	17. Staff regularly observe each other in the classroom and give each other feedback.	☐	☐	☐	☐	☐
	☐	☐	☐	☐	☐	18. Staff engage in team teaching as a way of improving practice.	☐	☐	☐	☐	☐
	☐	☐	☐	☐	☐	19. If staff have a problem with their teaching they usually turn to colleagues for help.	☐	☐	☐	☐	☐
	☐	☐	☐	☐	☐	20. Teachers suggest ideas or approaches for colleagues to try in class.	☐	☐	☐	☐	☐
	☐	☐	☐	☐	☐	21. Teachers make collective agreements to test out new ideas.	☐	☐	☐	☐	☐

SCALE X
This school now
(About your colleagues!)

SCALE Y
How important are these practices and beliefs for creating opportunities for pupils to learn?
(About your values)

True of no staff	True of few staff	True of some staff	True of most staff	Don't know	Professional learning practices and beliefs of colleagues	Not at all important	Of limited importance	Important	Crucial	Bad practice!
☐	☐	☐	☐	☐	22. Teachers discuss openly with colleagues what and how they are learning.	☐	☐	☐	☐	☐
☐	☐	☐	☐	☐	23. Staff frequently use informal opportunities to discuss how children learn.	☐	☐	☐	☐	☐
☐	☐	☐	☐	☐	24. Staff offer one another reassurance and support.	☐	☐	☐	☐	☐
☐	☐	☐	☐	☐	25. Staff believe that all pupils are capable of learning.	☐	☐	☐	☐	☐
☐	☐	☐	☐	☐	26. Pupils in this school enjoy learning.	☐	☐	☐	☐	☐
☐	☐	☐	☐	☐	27. Pupil success is regularly celebrated.	☐	☐	☐	☐	☐
☐	☐	☐	☐	☐	28. Staff discuss with colleagues how pupils might be helped to learn how to learn.	☐	☐	☐	☐	☐

Tool 2: Staff questionnaire C: School management practices and systems

Completing the questionnaire

1 Staff questionnaire C consists of 26 statements. Each statement relates to an aspect of school management practices and systems.

2 There are two scales for each of the items in section C: scale X and scale Y.

3 Scale X, on the left hand side, asks you to indicate whether and to what extent you think that particular management practices are carried out at any level of management in your school.

4 Scale Y, on the right hand side, asks you to indicate how important you regard each of the listed management practices and systems for creating opportunities for pupils to learn, irrespective of the extent to which you think that the practice is carried out at your school. Or, do you think a particular practice is simply bad practice? In this case you would tick the box in the fifth column in scale Y.

5 Tick only one box on scale X and one box on scale Y.

Example

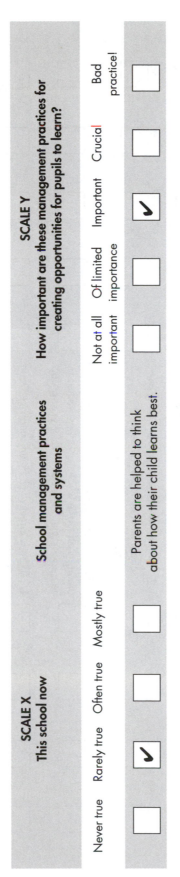

This respondent thinks that parents are rarely included in decision-making processes at this school but that inclusion of parents in decision-making plays an important role in enhancing pupils' learning.

Please complete the questionnaire now.

SCALE X — This school now				School management practices and systems	SCALE Y — How important are these management practices for creating opportunities for pupils to learn?				
Never true	Rarely true	Often true	Mostly true		Not at all important	Of limited importance	Important	Crucial	Bad practice!
☐	☐	☐	☐	1. Senior management communicates a clear vision of where the school is going.	☐	☐	☐	☐	☐
☐	☐	☐	☐	2. Staff have a commitment to the whole school as well as to their department, key stage and/or year group.	☐	☐	☐	☐	☐
☐	☐	☐	☐	3. Senior management promotes commitment among staff to the whole school as well as to the department, key stage and/or year group.	☐	☐	☐	☐	☐
☐	☐	☐	☐	4. There is effective communication between senior management and teachers.	☐	☐	☐	☐	☐
☐	☐	☐	☐	5. There are processes for involving all staff in decision-making.	☐	☐	☐	☐	☐
☐	☐	☐	☐	6. Teachers' professional know-how is used in the formulation of school policy and goals.	☐	☐	☐	☐	☐
☐	☐	☐	☐	7. Teachers' professional know-how is used in the formulation of school policy, even where this leads to a questioning of established rules, procedures and practices.	☐	☐	☐	☐	☐
☐	☐	☐	☐	8. Opportunities are provided for teachers to critically evaluate school policy.	☐	☐	☐	☐	☐

SCALE X
This school now

SCALE Y
How important are these management practices for creating opportunities for pupils to learn?

Never true	Rarely true	Often true	Mostly true	School management practices and systems	Not at all important	Of limited importance	Important	Crucial	Bad practice!
☐	☐	☐	☐	9. Staff are actively involved in evaluating school policy.	☐	☐	☐	☐	☐
☐	☐	☐	☐	10. Staff participate in important decision-making.	☐	☐	☐	☐	☐
☐	☐	☐	☐	11. There are processes for involving pupils in decision-making.	☐	☐	☐	☐	☐
☐	☐	☐	☐	12. Staff have a good working knowledge of the School Development Plan.	☐	☐	☐	☐	☐
☐	☐	☐	☐	13. Staff see the School Development Plan as relevant and useful to learning and teaching.	☐	☐	☐	☐	☐
☐	☐	☐	☐	14. Staff development time is used effectively to realise School Development Plan priorities.	☐	☐	☐	☐	☐
☐	☐	☐	☐	15. Staff development time is used effectively in the school.	☐	☐	☐	☐	☐
☐	☐	☐	☐	16. The school provides cover to allow staff joint planning time.	☐	☐	☐	☐	☐
☐	☐	☐	☐	17. Teachers are encouraged to experiment with new ideas as a way of promoting professional growth.	☐	☐	☐	☐	☐
☐	☐	☐	☐	18. Formal training provides opportunities for teachers to develop professionally.	☐	☐	☐	☐	☐

School management practices and systems

Scale X: This school now				School management practices and systems	Scale Y: How important				
Never true	Rarely true	Often true	Mostly true		Not at all important	Of limited importance	Important	Crucial	Bad practice!
☐	☐	☐	☐	19. Teachers are helped to develop skills to assess pupils' work in ways that move their pupils on in their learning.	☐	☐	☐	☐	☐
☐	☐	☐	☐	20. Teachers are helped to develop skills to observe learning as it happens in the classroom.	☐	☐	☐	☐	☐
☐	☐	☐	☐	21. Management supports teachers in sharing practice with other schools through networking.	☐	☐	☐	☐	☐
☐	☐	☐	☐	22. Information is collected from teachers on those aspects of their work that they themselves think they do effectively.	☐	☐	☐	☐	☐
☐	☐	☐	☐	23. Information is collected from teachers on effective ways they promote learning to learn skills and knowledge among their students.	☐	☐	☐	☐	☐
☐	☐	☐	☐	24. Information is collected from teachers on informal teacher networking in which they play an active role.	☐	☐	☐	☐	☐
☐	☐	☐	☐	25. Teacher-initiated networking is an integral element of staff development.	☐	☐	☐	☐	☐
☐	☐	☐	☐	26. Learning how to learn is an issue discussed in staff development time.	☐	☐	☐	☐	☐

Tool 3: Reflecting on the survey data

Purpose

This tool is a prompt designed to scan the staff questionnaire results, focusing on places where there are gaps between expectation and current practice, and then focusing on one or more areas for more detailed discussion and strategic planning.

Context

This could be used in a staff inset session to enable all staff to participate in a process of reflection and judgement about the implications of the survey data.

Procedure

Organise staff into trios. Give each group a copy of the raw data and the histograms for the Y–X differences which indicate gaps between practice and values. Ask that each trio has a scribe and give the scribes the tool.

Related factors

As it stands, the tool could be used to address all Staff questionnaire B ('Professional learning') and C ('School management and systems') factors, but it could be extended to cover A ('Classroom assessment') factors as well.

Prompts for reflection

1 Inquiry: learning from external sources (Factor B1)

This is about learning from practice in other schools and using research reports and websites to inform practice. It may also involve consulting pupils/students.

	No	A bit	Definitely
Does the survey data indicate a gap between what we value and what we actually do?			

How do we explain this gap? Is this a problem? Do we need to take action?

What kind of strategy could we adopt to address the problem?

Strategy	

2 Inquiry: learning from internal sources (Factor B1)

This is about looking at our practice through self-evaluation and feedback from pupils. It involves a deliberate attempt to modify practice and adapt it in the light of evidence.

	No	A bit	Definitely
Does the survey data indicate a gap between what we value and what we actually do?			

How do we explain this gap? Is this a problem? Do we need to take action?

What kind of strategy could we adopt to address the problem?

Strategy	

3 Building social capital, and critical and responsive learning (Factors B2 and B3)

This is about working together on planning and research or evaluation activities. It involves discussion of classroom practice, supporting each other and working on joint solutions to problems.

	No	A bit	Definitely
Does the survey data indicate a gap between what we value and what we actually do?			

How do we explain this gap? Is this a problem? Do we need to take action?

What kind of strategy could we adopt to address the problem?

Strategy	

4 Deciding and acting together (Factor C1)

This is about involving colleagues and students in decision-making and policy formation. It brings to bear everyone's expertise to create and to challenge policy.

	No	A bit	Definitely
Does the survey data indicate a gap between what we value and what we actually do?			

How do we explain this gap? Is this a problem? Do we need to take action?

What kind of strategy could we adopt to address the problem?

Strategy	

5 Developing a sense of where we are going (Factor C2)

This is about the extent to which there is a shared vision about the way the school is developing and how colleagues are using staff development time to further this shared vision.

	No	A bit	Definitely
Does the survey data indicate a gap between what we value and what we actually do?			

How do we explain this gap? Is this a problem? Do we need to take action?

What kind of strategy could we adopt to address the problem?

Strategy	

6 Auditing expertise and supporting networking (Factor C4)

This is about the opportunities that colleagues have to develop their skills and to share knowledge about practice through networking both within the school and with teachers in other schools.

	No	A bit	Definitely
Does the survey data indicate a gap between what we value and what we actually do?			

How do we explain this gap? Is this a problem? Do we need to take action?

What kind of strategy could we adopt to address the problem?

Strategy	

Tool 4: Snowballing: indicators of an LHTL culture

Purpose

This activity is designed to open a dialogue around the key factors embedded in/arising from the LHTL staff questionnaires. Through questioning, discussion and the attempt to find consensus or reasoned disagreement, participants are able to probe deeper into the nature of school culture and identify areas for improvement.

Context

The activity was designed originally for use by a governing body to find an engaging way into the issues and to give them a stake in the substantive debate about school improvement. It may be used by any group – parents, pupils, senior leadership, or staff on an INSET day.

Procedure

The table below contains key factors from both factor analysis and theoretical constructs, worded to make them meaningful for a governing body, parent group or any other relevant group.

These may each be rated on a four-point scale, say, or, alternatively, choose 5 from 10 and rank in order of importance from 1 to 5.

There are three stages:

1   individual (5–7 minutes)
2   pairs, three or fours (15 minutes)

3   whole group (20 minutes).

At stages 2 and 3 there must be an effort to reach consensus following these rules:

4   no insisting on your own position
5   listening carefully to other people's position
6   no trading ('I'll give you 3 if you let me have 4')
7   no averaging (add up scores and divide)
8   look for, and pay close attention to, evidence.

Related factors

Any one or all of the factors may be touched on, and one or two can then be focused on in greater depth. The activity itself addresses most centrally the factors:

B2 Building social capital
B3 Critical and responsive learning
C1 Deciding and acting together
C2 Developing a sense of where we are going.

Indicators of an LHTL culture	My view	Small-group view	Whole-group view
Pupils are clear about the purposes of what they are learning.			
Pupils are helped to become independent learners.			
Throughout the school, people research, inquire and reflect critically on practice.			
Teachers are open to change, but critical as to what is most important in terms of learning.			
Teachers in the school learn together, exchanging ideas and practice.			
There is a strong ethos of mutual support among staff.			
People talk about and value learning, not just grades, marks and test scores.			
This school is characterised by people deciding and acting together.			
There is a strong shared sense of where we are going as a school.			
All staff have opportunities for continuing professional development.			

Tool 5: The matrix

Purpose

This tool enables teachers to reflect on the school's culture. Its premise is that individual teachers may either privatise or share their thinking and practice (a broadening dimension) and/or may strengthen and enhance their practice (a deepening dimension). It is designed to provoke discussion on aspects of school life.

Context

The activity can be done individually or collectively, the collective dimension (deep and broad) being the goal of the LHTL school.

Procedure

This matrix may be used by a group of staff to consider how they see practice in their school. The workshop leader will need to explain the dimensions of the matrix.

> We may distinguish two implicit notions underlying the way in which capacity, or organisational capital, is discussed – in terms of broadening, and of deepening. *Broadening* capacity may be seen as bringing a greater sense of inclusiveness to current practice. In school improvement terms this might be translated as attenuating balkanisation, or bringing together smaller islands of practice to create a wider shared community of practice. This dimension may be described as 'density'. *Deepening* capacity may be seen as enabling teachers, individually or collectively, to dig beneath current practice and, through a more acute interrogation of what happens in the classroom, to extend the repertoire of thought and action. This provides a two-dimensional matrix which creates four broad typologies.

People may first work individually to plot where they see the school. This is likely to:

- generate different perceptions;
- bring the response that it depends on context, time or nature of the task;
- possibly create resistance or lead to the instrument being rejected.

All of these are worth exploring further but may require either a facilitator to help people to drop defensive attitudes and, if they choose:

- take a specific time or event in the life of the school to analyse in these terms;
- improve on the instrument;
- decide to use this framework to monitor what happens in the next week.

The LHTL school would be characterised by the elements in the top right quadrant, indications for which will be found through the questionnaire instrument and by revisiting this at a later stage in the school's development. A positive shift on factors, and on some specific items, will help to signal whether there is a growth in capacity. This may, of course, not represent a 'real' shift, as staff will not come to the questionnaire 'fresh', and will be more aware of the model and expectations. Follow-up exploration of responses will, therefore, be vital as well as drawing on other data sources.

The matrix

Deepening (high)

Strong on human capital. Teachers reflect on and research their own practice, some through further qualifications and sponsored research. Professional time is used for personal development. There is a high level of critical self-evaluation and many teachers show enthusiasm for a broader repertoire of evaluation and development tools. There is a variety of practice and values across the school.

Strong on social capital. Teachers routinely reflect critically on their practice, sharing their findings with others, triumphs as well as disasters. Evidence is sought and critically evaluated. People listen sensitively to one another but are not afraid to challenge. They routinely and informally visit one another's classrooms, exchanging ideas and resources. Values are discussed but differences are acknowledged and learned from. Ideas are evaluated on their merits without regard for status or hierarchy. There is shared responsibility for the induction of newly qualified teachers and classroom assistants.

Broadening (low)   Broadening (high)

There is a strong sense of individual autonomy. Teachers privatise their practice and jealously guard expertise and resources, investing their energies in their own class and their relationships with their own pupils. They disengage themselves from school-wide development if it is not seen as in the interest of their class or of direct relevance to teaching and learning.

There is a strong collegiate spirit in the school. Staff have pride in their school and see it is a good school whatever the outsiders' view. Teachers share ideas and practices and learn from one another. Staff have a strong sense of solidarity in evaluating and resisting change which is not widely agreed. They place a high premium on consensus and have low level of tolerance for idiosyncrasy and deviance.

Deepening (low)

Related factors

This activity contributes to addressing factors:

C1 Deciding and acting together
C2 Developing a sense of where we are going.

Tool 6: Through the eyes of the NQT

Purpose

This is an exercise to help a school see itself though fresh eyes. It confronts the school with the fresh perspective that an NQT can bring and helps staff to consider how it would answer these questions and what other questions might be added to the given list. The newly qualified teacher is bombarded with new information in the first few weeks and forms a host of impressions of the school. These are usually kept private but may be important sources of data. They are particularly relevant in a climate of a recruitment and retention 'crisis'. We may frame some questions in terms of ethos ('feel' and first impressions) and culture (deeper lying aspects of relationships and values).

Context

This may simply be used as a reference source, a backdrop to ongoing discussions in the school, and returned to from time to time. Alternatively, it may be used in a more structured way, as an agenda for discussion within a leadership team, a departmental staff or a group of teachers.

Procedure

In the context of a group discussion, say a group of five, each participant may be given the set of questions to answer from their individual standpoint, then come together as a group to share their analysis. This may include an NQT or NQTs if this is considered appropriate.

Related factors

While this activity relates most closely to factors in B, those of particular relevance are:

B1 Inquiry
C1 Deciding and acting together.

The questions

Ethos

- Do I feel welcome?
- Do I get help to find my way around?
- Am I treated as a fellow professional?
- Do pupils see me as just another member of staff?
- Am I listened to?
- Do I feel valued?

Culture

- Is this a school that will recognise the knowledge and expertise that I already possess?
- Will it value the special talents and assets that I bring with me?
- Will it appreciate the optimism and expectation that have led me to make this commitment?
- Will it acknowledge my self-doubt and allow me to fail as well as providing the best conditions for success?
- Will it allow me to share openly with others what I have done well and help me feel free to admit to private disasters?
- Will I have the occasion to observe and learn from others and will they be professional enough to observe and learn from me?
- Is this a school in which people talk about learning on a daily basis?
- Does the headteacher and leadership team believe they can learn from the most junior staff member?
- Is this a school in which I will be encouraged to grow and develop professionally?

Tool 7: Critical incident analysis

Purpose

This tool is used to help people examine aspects of school culture through the analysis of critical events in the life of the school. How people respond to an event may powerfully illuminate how the school learns and draws lessons from individual and group behaviour.

Context

A group (senior leadership team, a working party, governors, school council) or mixed group of staff in a CPD session, for example, choose a recent event in the life of the school. It might be a disciplinary incident, a newspaper report, a complaint from the community, an adverse inspection. This provides the focus for a close examination of what happened (different accounts are likely to emerge): What was the context? What preceded? What followed? Who were the key players? What might we do differently next time?

Procedure

As a group, people go back through the incident in as much descriptive detail as they can recall.

- Suspend judgement. Don't allocate blame.
- Don't argue for your construction of the event. Listen to others.
- Describe from an objective, disinterested viewpoint what happened.
- Try to remember the conditions – e.g. time of day, the weather (was it raining? hot? etc.), preceding events.
- Who was involved (the cast)?
- What did different people do? And not do?
- What was said?

People's memories, or constructions, of the event will be different. This is an important aspect of the exercise and should be recorded in some way. It may hold the key to the way in which people respond, allocate responsibility and decide on a course of action.

Having agreed, as far as possible, what happened, now reflect on questions such as:

- Who was involved?
- What might have been done differently?
- What were the possible options? (Allow for wild ideas.)
- Who held the options?
- Why were they not used? (Avoid blame or judgement.)
- What have we learned from the incident?
- What might we do differently next time?

The figure overleaf shows an example from a group of Year 9 girls in a London school.

The cast

- pupil
- rest of the class
- teacher
- parent
- headteacher.

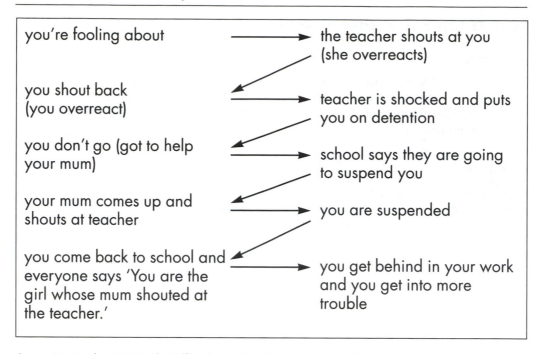

Source: MacBeath, J. (2003) *The Self-Evaluation File*. Glasgow, Learning Files Scotland.

Options

Pupil: Stop mucking about. Apologise.
Rest of class: Take responsibility. Try to stop things getting out of hand.
Teacher: Stay calm. Be firm. Don't overreact. Don't victimise.
Parent: Find out what happened.
Headteacher: Sort things out before they go too far.

Related factors

While this activity relates to a wide range of factors, those most relevant to this activity may focus on:

B1 Inquiry
C1 Deciding and acting together.

Tool 8: Leadership density analysis

Purpose

If we really believe that shared leadership can help to improve learning, we need to explore what is involved in exercising leadership. Then we need to ask the following question: To what extent can members of the school community and the school's community have influence over what happens in school?

We could say that all of the categories of people listed below can exercise leadership. They all have *values* which underpin their *vision* of how things ought to be and they can all take *action* which *influences* what happens in school.

- pupils
- teachers
- middle leaders
- headteachers
- other staff (including catering, administrators/clerical workers, learning support people)
- parents
- community stakeholders (leaders of religious or ethnic groups, employers, youth workers).

Not everyone has the same expectation about exercising leadership and these groups have different expectations of one another. Not everyone has the same capacity for leadership. Some are more strategic than others. Some exercise leadership in a very negative or irresponsible way, but everyone has influence. The outcomes – what actually happens – are the result of 'conjoint agency'.

If schools want to build their capacity for sustained improvement, they need to consider the extent to which the people listed above are able to have influence within a framework of responsibility and mutual accountability. We can use the matrix to explore why people might find it difficult to have influence. We are then in a position to address these difficulties.

Context

The matrix could be used by the senior leadership team in order to make a judgement about where to target action. It could also be used as a staff development activity for the whole staff to stimulate collective reflection on the state of the school as an innovative or transformational organisation.

Procedure

If the material is to be used in a staff development workshop, it should be explained or suggested that the categories of people listed actually do exercise leadership although they may not think of it in these terms.

Following this introduction to the idea, participants will need to be talked through the sheet which explains the factors affecting the capacity to exercise leadership. Then the matrix can be distributed with some explanation for the groups of people: headteachers, teachers, other staff (including learning support assistants, catering and administrative staff), pupils, parents, and community stakeholders (e.g. leaders of religious or ethnic groups, employers, youth workers).

Related factors

This activity would contribute to addressing factors:

B2 Building social capital
B3 Critical and responsive learning
C1 Deciding and acting together, and
C2 Developing a sense of where we are going.

Leadership density analysis

To what extent can members of the school community have influence over what happens in school?
(Score: 0 = none; 1 = weak; 2 = moderate; 3 = strong)

	Pupils	Teachers	Headteachers	Middle leaders	Support staff	Parents	Other stakeholders
Authority							
Pedagogic knowledge							
Community networks							
Organisational knowledge							
ICT expertise							
Change champions							
Leadership capacity							

Factors affecting the capacity to exercise leadership

Expectations

To what extent do people feel that they have the right to have influence? To what extent do people allow or expect others to have influence? In what areas do people feel that they should have influence? These expectations clearly shape the capacity to have influence.

Organisational structures

The structures and procedure through which a school is managed may enable various categories of people to exercise leadership. Opportunities to contribute and to express a view will vary. What structures might help different members of the school community to exercise leadership?

The organisational culture

The system of values, beliefs and normal ways of behaving make up the organisational culture of the school. This culture will shape the extent to which various stakeholders can exercise leadership. How does the culture support or inhibit the exercise of leadership?

Social capital

This is the degree of trust that exists between members of an organisation. People are more able to influence each other when there are good social relationships and a high degree of trust. How can social capital be built up so that leadership density is maximised?

Authority/power

Those in formal positions may have some obvious forms of material power, for example the control of funds, but mostly people have influence because of their authority rather than their power. People within the school community have different types of authority or can draw upon different sources of authority. For example, a head of department may have bureaucratic authority, a teacher may have 'professional authority' because of their classroom expertise, or a parent or a student may be able to draw on 'moral authority'.

Knowledge about teaching and learning

We assume that teachers know about teaching and learning and they are sometimes defensive about this specialist knowledge, but pedagogical knowledge is contentious and others have views. For example, the government may promulgate particular beliefs and practices; pupils have immense experience of so many classrooms and will have insights to offer; parents will have experience, insights and beliefs about teaching and learning. How can knowledge about teaching and learning be used in the exercise of leadership?

Knowledge of the school as an organisation

We might expect headteachers to have more of this than anyone else. It is an important variable – knowing how the organisation is built and how it works enables you to be strategic in having influence. How can we address the lack of organisational knowledge that prevents some members of the school community from having influence?

Knowledge of the community

This term refers to what we know about the community that surrounds the school and from which the students are drawn. Some people are well informed about patterns of friendship, employment opportunities, ethnic groupings, tensions between social groups, and incidents and dramas in the community. How can this knowledge be used for the benefit of the school community?

Interpersonal skills

Another key variable is our competence in being able to form and sustain collaborative relationships. This involves a repertoire of skills and strategies for working with others. How can different categories of people develop the interpersonal skills which they need in order to 'win friends and influence people'?

Tool 9: Leadership tasks

Purpose

This card-based discussion activity enables teachers to explore the tasks involved in the exercise of leadership or undertaking the role of change agent.

Context

It is probably most suitable as a workshop activity for co-ordinators.

Procedure

Organise participants into groups of no more than five. The group(s) should be asked to sort and evaluate the cards. This can be done in a number of ways; two suggestions are given here.

1 Put the cards in a single pile, face downwards. Each person in turn picks up the top card and comments on it: whether they would do this, whether it is a good strategy for supporting change, and so on. Other members of the group may wish to add comments. The group may then place the card in an 'accept' or 'reject' pile. Once all the cards have been discussed and sorted, the group can then look at the accepted cards and try to agree on a statement that sums up their values and views about managing change. If there are several groups, these statements can be shared and discussed at the end.

2 Place the cards face upwards on a table and ask the group to arrange them in a shape that represents their values and views about leading and managing change. The search for consensus will lead to a discussion about the value of different strategies. When completed, a spokesperson for the group should explain the pattern to the group leader and if appropriate to the other groups.

Leadership tasks		
Co-ordinate the activities of individuals.	Bid for required resources.	Provide clear leadership.
Make contacts with outside agencies and other schools.	Stimulate discussion on key issues.	Define the objectives clearly.
Organise regular and effective meetings.	Provide links to useful sources of expertise.	Provide a forum for discussion and debate.
Help colleagues to analyse current practice.	Explain new ideas to colleagues in a rational and persuasive way.	Clarify the issues for colleagues.
Be exemplary.	Facilitate the growth of trust between colleagues.	Give colleagues clear indications of weaknesses in their current practices.
Give colleagues clear indications of ways in which their practice could be improved.	Help colleagues to identify their strengths.	Facilitate self-evaluation.
Encourage better working relationships between team members.	Provide anxious colleagues with reassurance.	Share your own strengths and weaknesses.
Evaluate colleagues' progress.	Bid for time to devote to team deliberations.	Organise and lead staff development activities.
Promote colleagues' confidence and self-esteem.	Give colleagues praise and recognition for any positive development.	Provide information about new ideas and developments.

Related factors

This activity may contribute to addressing factor.

C2 Developing a sense of where we are going.

Tool 10: Peer observation

Purpose

Peer observation is used primarily for teachers to reflect together on practice, to identify strategies for improvement, and to consider ways of sharing that knowledge more
widely.

Peer observation is generally welcomed by teachers because its focus is not on
accountability but improvement. It is invitational rather than mandated, negotiated
rather than imposed, focused on what the teacher chooses rather than what is chosen
by the observer.

Context

This is a collegial classroom-based activity agreed between two or more teachers. Two
teachers, for example, agree to observe one another, A visiting B's classroom with a
return visit by B to A at another date. This could be a group of three teachers agreeing
on a schedule of mutual visits. These may be within a department or cross depart-
mentally. The latter is more valuable from an LHTL whole-school perspective because
it begins to identify generic principles and generic examples of more effective practice.

Procedures

The teacher invites a colleague to observe a lesson or sequence within a lesson. The
teacher has in mind an issue on which she would like to get feedback. The observer
listens, perhaps probes further or suggests a procedure. Both agree on:

- what will be observed
- the time frame
- the timing and nature of the feedback
- what will be said to the class about the observer.

The following illustrates the process:

Teacher 1:   I would like you to focus on my use of the 'no hands up except to ask a question' rule. I
feel I am not very successful in breaking old habits.

Teacher 2:   So what would you like me to do?

Teacher 1:   I'd like you to do two things if you would. First, observe the introduction to the lesson
when I'm explaining the purposes and setting the context of the lesson. This is usually all
me talking and no-one ever puts their hands up . . .

Teacher 2:   And that is when you would *like* them to be putting their hands up . . .

Teacher 1:   Yes, but they don't. So what is it that I'm doing, or not doing that inhibits them asking
questions or volunteering?

Teacher 2:   And perhaps not just what you're doing or not doing but what else might be going on
in the class. Or might it be because you are the only one in the school doing this?

Teacher 1:   Well, that may be an explanation I guess, but I don't want to lose the focus on what I'm
doing, or not, so I can get some idea of how to change my behaviour . . . and change
theirs.

Teacher 2: 'So focus on things like body language and actual language, and pace and . . .?'
Teacher 1: 'Whatever . . .'

And so on.

At the end of the lesson the observer asks the teacher to start with her own observation before feeding back what she had noted. The feedback is mainly descriptive rather than evaluative, describing what the teacher did, but offering some more tentative observations on what she perceived regarding:

- tone of voice
- language register
- body language
- eye contact
- rhythm and pauses in speech
- explicit invitation to comment or question
- implicit invitation to comment or question.

This is followed by a dialogue on the potential effects of any of these things in isolation or in combination.

- What have both learned?
- What is worth sharing with our colleagues?
- What will we do next?

Related factors

While this activity relates to a wide range of factors, those most relevant to this activity are:

B1 Inquiry
C3 Supporting professional development.

Tool 11: Recasting outcomes

Purpose

This activity asks people to take a critical view of outcome measures, language and underpinning assumptions about outcomes. Its purpose is to help reframe how people view essential purposes, processes and structures of the LHTL school.

Context

This activity may be used with staff on an INSET session or in any other setting where people are reflecting on priorities, self-evaluation, development planning, reporting or preparation for inspection.

Procedure

The list below provides examples of outcomes, and putative outcomes, from the ESRC project 'Consulting Pupils about their Learning'. These may provide a useful starting point for discussion on:

- the currency of these as 'outcomes'
- how they might be measured and reported.

Outcomes

- pupils' changing attitudes to school
- pupils' changed perceptions of teachers
- teachers' changing perceptions of young people
- a stronger sense of membership among pupils
- a stronger sense of collegiality/shared learning among teachers
- pupils' capacity for perspective taking
- teachers' capacity for perspective taking
- pupils' developing capacity to talk about learning
- pupils' developing capacity to talk about teaching
- pupils' changed attitude to learning
- sharing and dialogue about purposes of learning and teaching
- teachers changing their thinking and practice.

Related factors

B4   Valuing learning
B2   Critical and responsive learning
C2   Developing a sense of where we're going.

Tool 12: Network-mapping

Purpose

This tool is designed to allow respondents to visualise the networks that their school is part of, through considering the communications in which the organisation is involved. It allows schools to reflect critically on these connections and consider where they might be strengthened for added value.

Context

In the LHTL project, the tool was used in one-to-one interviews with school leaders. The researcher helped the map compiler with standardised prompts. On one occasion a researcher administered this task to a group of map compilers. It was also used remotely, but less successfully, by sending instructions to individuals who compiled maps in their own time. The facilitator will need to think of the intended use of the task and tailor the process accordingly. Guidance to the facilitator and ideas of what to say to the map compiler are given below. The task will be of most benefit if it can be revisited at a later date to evaluate change.

Procedure

We suggest using a four-stage process and working through an example first. The first two stages are concerned with how to generate a network map. The final stages involve map analysis and map review.

Related factors

B2   Building social capital
C4   Auditing expertise and supporting networking.

Network mapping instrument

Stage 1: trying out your ideas

Note to facilitator: This stage should take 10–15 minutes. Structured brainstorming is recommended to help the map compilers order their thoughts. This is important because this task is asking them to bring together complex information.

First decide how to represent the people, groups, organisations and communities (to be called *nodes*) you communicate with. You may want to consider *where* you communicate (these places also being nodes) and certainly *how* you communicate or have a relationship with them (to be called *links*). You should also consider how often/*when* the connections are made. You may need to develop a key for both links and nodes. Start by jotting down, in any way that makes sense to you, who, when, where and how you consider communications to happen. Use a separate sheet, just to develop your ideas before starting the map itself.

Stage 2: producing the main map

Note to facilitator: This stage should take 20–30 minutes. You will need to set the task and could use the guideline prompts below. It was found when trialing this tool that more information on nodes and links was collected by recording a commentary of people talking through the process of drawing a map. If you are working with an individual, asking them to explain their thinking as they draw the map may help you to prompt them appropriately. Repeat the prompts given below and, for specific links, ask for more information on who, when, where and how they are communicating. The final 5–10 minutes could be spent asking for a five point bullet-point oral summary of what issues (values and attitudes) they perceived to affect the activity and roles being represented and perhaps what they found difficult to represent.

Take the A3 sheet and choose a way to lay out and represent the nodes and links you have considered. Start thinking about *internal* communications first and ask yourself

- Who are the key people?
- What are the key roles?
- Where are the key places?
- When are the key times?
- Which are they key methods?

Then think about *external* connections, asking yourself the same questions. Consider:

- the local community
- the local educational community
- national connections and even, perhaps, international ones.

Remember this is *your* view of the connections and may include what may at first glance seem incidental, informal, chance encounters or very personal relationships, but this is your chance to show how these may be nevertheless important to the flows of information, advice and collaborative activities that you are aware of.

Finally, go back and check you have expressed *how* these communications take place.

- Have you represented the frequency of the communications?
- Can you show the strength of the relationships?
- Are they all bi-directional or are some only one-way?

Stage 3: analysis

Analysis of each map allows the map compiler and those interested in the evidence of the map to categorise patterns of interaction. This provides an opportunity to reflect on everyday communications and consider aspects such as time management, the location of expertise, knowledge flow and to plan effective management of the networks.

The analysis and review stages will depend heavily on time allocated. The LHTL project was able to devote researcher time to complete a feedback form for every map and return this to the map compiler in advance of a final interview. This involved descriptive or first-level analysis. The form is to be found overleaf and its use is fairly straightforward. Those using the tool would need to decide the form of analysis and when and how it could be undertaken. Within the LHTL project, a further, second-level, inferential, analysis was undertaken by a team of project researchers (Carmichael, 2006).

Note to facilitator: If you have budgeted time, this stage can be an individual task for the map compiler, and will take at least 1 hour. Which categorisation of nodes and links you choose will depend on the most relevant to your own purposes for carrying out the task. If you were working with a group of map compilers, this stage could be adapted for working in pairs and looking at each other's maps. You could discuss these qualitatively with respect to one categorisation method for nodes and one for links. This descriptive analysis may be useful in making sense of the map and could be useful for comparison either laterally, if several of you are doing these, or temporally, if you want to revisit the map at a later date.

After the map has been drawn you may want to extract and allocate the nodes/links to categories considering any combination of the methods below:

- nodes by type (categories: named people, roles, groups, organisations, communities);
- nodes by proximity (categories: internal, community-based, local educational community-based, national or international);
- identify key events and key places;
- list the links (node to node connections) according to the main methods of communication (categories: face-to-face, email, paper-based, telephone). By calculating the numbers of links in various categories, as a percentage of the total number of links, you can find out the spread of use of different communication methods. For example, you might find that 80 per cent of communications are face-to-face;
- list the links according to their strength (strong or weak)/directionality (one- or two-way) or frequency (daily, weekly, termly, annually, rarely).

Stage 4: discussion

Note to facilitator: In addition to using maps (and their summary) to address the focus you agreed at the outset, allow the map compiler time to discuss how comfortable they feel with the map, i.e. how well they feel it represents their awareness of activities. Which things did they find it difficult to represent? Would this be a useful visual to explain the connectivity and activitiy of the organisation or is it so personal that it is really a better representation of the individual's role and activity in the organisation? Does it portray the work of the individual?

You could both come back to the map later, perhaps after a change in role or at the end of a term to look for changes in either nodes or links.

If comparing maps between individuals you could look for similarities and differences, allowing you to answer questions such as: 'Are individuals drawing on different sources? 'Do some individuals have a unique knowledge of some activities?' or 'Could this be useful information to other members of the group?'

Form for generating descriptive analysis of network maps

Nodes

Type of node (number =)

Roles	no. of references
(list)	
People (named)	no. of references
(list)	
Groups	no. of references
(list)	
Organisations	no. of references
(list)	
Communities	no. of references
(list)	
Constructs (not specific entities)	no. of references
(list)	

Proximity

Local (immediate)
(list)
Local (educational)
(list)
Local (community)
(list)
National
(list)
International
(list)

Key people

(list)

Temporary activities

(list)

Key places

(list)

Key events

(list)

Links

Method of communication used (number of links =)

Face-to-face (meetings, visits, participation in conferences, training):	% of each
Paper-based:	% of each
Telephone:	% of each
Electronic (email):	% of each
Website use:	% of each
Others mentioned by respondent:	% of each

Direction of communication between nodes

None:	% of each
One way:	% of each
Two way:	% of each

Reference

See Carmichael, P., Fox, A., McCormick, R., Procter, R. and Honour, L. (2006) Teachers' networks in and out of school, *Research Papers in Education*, 21(2), pp. 217–234.

Part IV Developing and sharing practice

Developing AfL practice

In this section of the book, we present two examples of how teachers can develop and share practice. The first, 'Traffic lights', shows how a simple strategy, informed by AfL principles, evolved in different ways; the second, 'Pupil conferences', describes how a group of teachers in one local authority came up with a strategy for sharing and dissemination which put children very much at the centre.

'Traffic lights'

Peer- and self-assessment (see Part I of this book) does not necessarily have to focus on achievement against criteria of successful performance; instead, pupils can be encouraged to assess levels of confidence – particularly about problematic knowledge or 'threshold concepts' (those on which many others are built).

The principle

One approach is to use 'traffic lights'. The 'version' of this strategy which we advocate involves the teacher identifying a small number of objectives for the lesson which are made as clear as possible. At the end of the lesson, or at any appropriate point during it, pupils can then be asked to indicate, by a green, orange or red circle on their work, whether they feel a high, medium or low level of *confidence* in their learning related to each objective. The most valuable aspect of the strategy is the fact that it forces the pupil to reflect on what she or he has been learning, rather than being concerned solely with task completion and extrinsic rewards.

Creative development: 'traffic lights', smiley faces and furrowed brows

The principle of using 'traffic lights' to communicate levels of confidence in learning has been adopted by many schools. However, we found that teachers were imaginatively adapting the basic principle according to classroom context and age of the pupils. Examples included:

- 'Traffic lights' were replaced by 'smiley (or other) faces'. Partly a pragmatic response to the fact that not every child had green, orange and red pencils available, faces could be drawn (in ordinary pencil) showing faces varying in their 'happiness' and confidence. Pupils were also able to express a wider range of responses, including faces with furrowed brows indicating 'this is difficult, but I'm thinking very hard', and they could adjust facial expressions once problems had been addressed and their confidence raised.

- Teachers found that young children were sometimes unsure as to when they should use the 'orange' indicator. They found that even a two-fold version with only green and red still had the desired effect of causing children to stop and reflect on their work and their understanding.

- Teachers developed versions of 'traffic lights' to monitor work in progress, often providing children with a set of coloured cards which children would place beside them as they worked. Rather than responding to children's 'hands up', teachers intervened when they saw individuals or groups of children displaying their red cards.

- Other teachers adapted this approach for whole-class discussions and 'plenary' sessions. Again, pupils were provided with coloured cards which they were able to display either at appropriate review points, or at any time when they felt that they were 'losing track'. Some teachers described how they made children display the cards in such a way that their peers could not see them – avoiding the possibility of embarrassment or peer pressure.

- A primary teacher reported how the process had become so well-established that the need for 'props' had disappeared – although the principle of reflection was preserved. She describes how 'During my plenary session, I then ask them to think about how well they think they have achieved the objective. They can either be really confident and ready to move on, fairly confident and happy that they have more or less achieved the objective, or not ready to move on and need more help/practice. I turn my head, count to three and ask my class to be ready with a big smile, a straight face, or a frown, depending on how they feel. The kids love it, and because they are all facing me, they don't feel worried about their peers seeing their expressions. The grins are getting cheesier and the brows more furrowed in the frowns!'

Using 'traffic lights' formatively – and a note of caution

All of these versions of this simple reflective strategy can provide useful feedback to the teacher at two levels – to see if there are parts of the lesson that it would be worth re-doing with the whole class, but also to get feedback about which pupils would particularly benefit from individual support.

Some teachers went further and used the pupils' self-assessment of confidence as the basis of class groupings, asking ambers and greens to work together in pairs, while the teacher or a teaching assistant worked with the reds. In other schools, teachers have been adapting their 'threefold differentiation' of learning activities so that it can be used to respond to pupil self-assessment of confidence rather than being based on progress against curricular criteria.

All of these approaches, even those which have diverged from and developed the original strategy, retain a commitment to the principle of using 'traffic lights' to encourage reflection amongst pupils and teachers alike. Aside from adherence to this principle, there is no 'right' way – there is no 'best practice' in the use of 'traffic lights'. That said, the approach is not designed to be just another form of scoring, marking or grading, and the display of a red card, or the appearance of a furrowed brow (on a cartoon or a real child), should always be an signal that support is needed, rather than a mark of failure.

Sharing AfL practice

Pupil conferences

In one of the local authorities participating in the project a 'networked learning community' took AfL as its focus for school-based development work. Teachers from over twenty primary and secondary schools met over a two-year period to share ideas and experience, organise programmes of lesson observation and develop AfL strategies at classroom and school level.

A culture of sharing led to the production of:

- a website with examples of AfL practice for teachers within and beyond the local authority to try;
- an AfL handbook bringing together project materials and examples of practice developed in schools;
- resources designed to help teachers embed AfL practice into their lesson, termly, departmental and school development plans;
- a growing list of teachers who welcome visits to their classrooms by others interested in AfL.

Perhaps the most novel strategy to have developed, however, is the 'pupil conference' – a day event at which pupils from primary and secondary schools come together with teachers. They discuss their experiences of learning and strategies which they have found useful when applied in their schools. The focus is very clearly on what teachers and schools can do to help children learn, and the teachers who act as facilitators of discussions know that they are there to hear what children have to say – not to teach, train or advise them.

At the end of the conference, it is the children who return to their schools ready to report back on what they have heard and to share ideas with teachers as to what strategies they might adopt. Pupil conferences have been running for two years across the local authority, and individual schools are now beginning to adopt this approach; they have also attracted a good deal of media attention. Perhaps the most telling development, though, is that in the first pupil conference in 2004, the 'keynote' presentation was made by a member of the Learning How to Learn Project team; in 2005, the 'keynote speakers' were children from schools in the network.

'Traffic lights' again!

At the 2005 conference, pupils from participating schools were asked to assess formatively their schools' support for their learning and to make suggestions as to how they (the schools) might improve. Amongst their suggestions, one which attracted the widest support was that every child in the LA should have a set of 'traffic lights' on a key ring for use whenever required. A production run of 60,000 sets of 'traffic light' cards will ensure this is indeed the case for the new school year in 2005–2006. These cards – tools – will, of course, only be as good as the purposes to which they are put. Again the object of helping pupils, and their teachers, to become autonomous, independent learners, through reflection and self-regulation will be the guiding principle.

Appendix

About the Learning How to Learn project

'Learning How to Learn – in classrooms, schools and networks' was a development and research project funded as part of the Economic and Social Research Council's Teaching and Learning Research Programme (see http://www.tlrp.org). The project involved a team from four universities (Cambridge, King's College London, Reading and the Open University) working with forty primary and secondary schools in five local authorities (LAs) and one Virtual Education Action Zone (VEAZ) in England from 2001 to 2005. A general account of the research design, methods and findings of this project will be found in another book published by Routledge, entitled *Improving Learning How to Learn in Classrooms, Schools and Networks*, and in a special issue of the journal, *Research Papers in Education*, volume 21, number 2, 2006.

As a project within the Teaching and Learning Research Programme, we were expected to conduct research aimed at enhancing outcomes for learners in authentic settings. Whilst we wanted to produce high-quality research, we also wanted to produce findings that would be practically useful to teachers and schools. This book is one way of disseminating to teachers what we did, and what we found out, in the hope that it will help them to improve their practice for the benefit of their pupils.

We chose to build on previous research and development of formative assessment which demonstrated the promise of AfL for improved learning and achievement. However, this previous research was mostly conducted on a small scale with intensive support from researchers. If such innovations are to go 'system-wide' we knew that they would need to be implemented in real-world settings with much less support. Thus we chose to provide little more than the kind of help schools might find within their LA or from their own resources. Then we observed what happened. We were especially interested in how the project 'landed in schools' and why innovation 'took off' in one context but not another. Our particular interest was in the conditions within schools and networks that are conducive to the 'scaling up' and 'rolling out' of AFL and LHTL practice.

Development work in schools was initiated by the academics, who were the schools' 'critical friends', with the help of LA advisers who acted as local co-ordinators. External support was light-touch to simulate the kind of resource that schools might have available. Whole-school INSET introduced teachers to the evidence base; this was important in convincing them that AfL was worth trying. Then we shared with them some of the practical strategies that other schools had developed. Here we drew on evidence from Black and Wiliam's 1998 research review, their follow-up King's, Medway, Oxfordshire Formative Assessment Project, and a programme for school improvement that colleagues from Cambridge University had worked on with Hertfordshire schools.

An audit and action-planning activity enabled teachers to discuss how they would like to take the project forward in their schools. Some chose to work though optional workshops that we provided; others selected or adapted them. Each school decided how best to implement innovations. The other main intervention from the project team was to feed back to the school co-ordinator, and sometimes other staff, the results of the baseline survey we conducted into staff values and stated practices. This showed up differences among groups of staff and stimulated discussion and action. We provided materials to support more general professional development and school improvement strategies. At network level, school co-ordinators' meetings also provided development opportunities. An innovative website was created to aid communications between researchers and schools, and with a wider audience of interested individuals and groups.

Our research used careful and systematic data collection and analysis to enable us to analyse patterns across our sample as a whole, and over time, and to examine school differences on common measures. We developed research instruments at each level (classrooms, schools and networks) with a view to integrating them to provide a holistic picture. We also wanted to develop the kind of instruments that we could leave behind for school self-evaluation. We collected quantitative data, mainly through questionnaire surveys, to give us evidence of general patterns, associations, group differences and change over time. We collected qualitative data, mainly through recorded observations and interviews, to give us more depth of insight and especially to help us interpret statistical associations. We also requested performance data from national databases in order to provide some response to the question: Has the project observed improvements in pupils' measured attainments? As might be expected, the answer was 'Yes and No'. There were some notable successes and our case studies focus on exploring explanations for these, although we are careful not to make premature judgements about what precise features of schools, or the project, contribute to these effects.

Alongside this empirical work we also developed our conceptual understanding. One key aim was to extend work on AfL into a 'model of learning how to learn for both pupils and teachers'. We did not have a satisfactory definition of LHTL at the beginning of our work – which is why this was one of our aims. We are now clear that learning how to learn is not an entity or ability; neither can it be separated from learning, i.e. from learning something. Rather it is a family of learning *practices* that enable learning to happen. Thus we prefer 'learning how to learn' to 'learning to learn' – the *how* word seems important.

A second point on which we are clear is that learning independence, autonomy, or agency, has priority. This underpins AfL practice. Those who write about learning (how) to learn, from whatever intellectual base, emphasise the importance of self-direction and self-regulation. But they do not assume this is simply an individual characteristic. The social/collaborative dimension of learning is crucial. And this is true for both pupils and teachers. Evidence for these ideas has also emerged from our data.

Resources on the project website

Versions of most of the materials in this book have been placed on the Learning How to Learn Project website and can be downloaded: http://www.learntolearn.ac.uk. This website is also accessible from the Teaching and Learning Research Programme – http://www.tlrp.org – follow the links to 'Projects', then 'Across school phases'.

On the website you will find a range of resources including PowerPoint versions of the initial INSET presentation, workshop materials in versions for participants and facilitators, the learning at school level tool set, and research instruments that may be used for self-evaluation, along with some analytic tools. There is also an area, 'Assessment for Learning in Action', where teachers are encouraged to share information about how they have developed practice in their schools. In addition, the website contains general information about the project and details of other project publications as they emerge.

Index